Here's What P9-CCC-612

"Beverly Beyer has again updated and expanded her invaluable little book ... a discriminating selection of some 800 small hotels, castles, country inns, farms, old coaching stops, converted abbeys and monasteries — a goldmine of best buys for the budget traveler. She covers 500 cities, towns and resort villages in 23 countries" *Chicago Sun-Times*

"The best reference of its kind in print. It'll save you a bundle" *Los Angeles Times*

"Miss Beyer's selections are still made primarily for their comfort and value" *Baltimore Sun*

"Small, centrally located 'little grand hotels'" *Philadelphia Inquirer*

"Her personal guide offers the budget tourist suggestions for making a vacation more rewarding and less costly" *Kansas City Star*

"Adventurous but inexpensive nights ... Passport size — to sneak out of pockets and purses without looking like a greenhorn tourist" *Glamour*

"A little gem. One can enjoy excellent accommodations and cuisine without paying premium prices" *Library Journal*

PASSPORT

To Europe's
Small Hotels & Inns

Beverly Beyer

E.A. Rabey, Editor

John Wiley & Sons, Inc./A Passport Publications Book

New York/Chichester/Brisbane/Toronto/Singapore

Library of Congress Cataloging in Publication Data

Beyer, Beverly.
    Passport to Europe's small hotels & inns.

    (A Passport publications book)
    Includes index.
    1. Hotels, taverns, etc. — Europe — Directories.
I. Rabey, E. A. II. Title.
TX910.A1B48 1983   647'.94401   82-24704
ISBN 0-471-88960-1

Contents

To Palmer, who first showed promise with her report on San Gimignano's delightful La Cisterna at age four:
> *"nice hotel. has beds and CAT"*

Hotel drawings by John Caveny-Brown

Introduction

Nothing delights a traveler to Europe quite so much as "discovering" a small, comfortable and very fetching hotel or inn tucked away in the narrow streets of a Continental city or hidden behind the hedgerows, bramble and wildflowers lining a country lane.

After three decades of European travel I still feel a surge of excitement and expectation upon walking into such a place, particularly if its room rates are reasonable, reception desk smiles are warm and aromas from the kitchen waft a gentle cloud of temptation my way.

It matters little to me that Roman soldiers might have found it first, or that knights of the Second Crusade stabled their horses in the inn's courtyard. A pair of audacious 17th-century smugglers could very well have shared the same room that I had overlooking the rugged coast of Cornwall.

What's important is that I have found another lodging for the night that suits my fancy and, with luck, will suit yours.

Sometime between birth and our first passport picture an invisible hand reaches down from on high and stamps each of us with an equally invisible brand. Thenceforth and forever we are consigned to be one of two types of travelers.

One group seeks out the very newest high-rise hotel where carpets are endless, elevators swift and air conditioning turns balmy Greek evenings and crisp Irish mornings into one and the same. The other group invariably finds its deepest satisfaction before the welcoming hearth of a cozy small hotel or inn.

Alas, in all these years of travel I have been neither willing nor able to desert Group Two. And by buying and using this book, you may consider yourself an accredited member of our happy band.

This year marks the 23rd annual edition of our book and during those years we have tried never to lose sight of the particular type reader we had in mind at the outset. Thousands of letters, some from travelers using their sixth or eighth edition, have convinced us that our point-of-view was right for this book in 1960 and for our other travel books published in later years.

Our reader, bless him, is an adventurer. While he may splurge occasionally by going first-cabin, there is always a *rucksack* in his soul. He is footloose, independent and — whether he's been to Europe or not — just as anxious to visit the hill towns of Tuscany as sit on Rome's Via Veneto. Everything indicates that he is also a reasonably knowledgeable traveler. We can't remember ever receiving a question about passports, shots or the comparative sizes of German shoes, answers he gets sensibly from the nearest post office, his doctor or a German shoe salesman.

Besides, all this information takes valuable space — plus adding weight for you to carry around Europe. Our aim continues to be to offer a book of essential hotel information for the traveler, one that will fit your pocket or purse yet give hotel prices that are as current as our year-end press time will allow.

Yet our readers do ask questions. Some of them we can answer. And for others, we refer you to sources that we know have better, more up-to-date answers. For that reason we are again expanding our introduction to include a combination of the two.

Another major addition is the thumbnail sketch before each country. While we are still not attempting to be a comprehensive guide, these brief introductory paragraphs will let you know something of what to expect upon arrival in a particular country. Currency, food, car rental and fuel costs, rail and bus transportation, offbeat regions or provinces that you may not know of, something of the people themselves. In short, an effort to make your arrival and visit both comfortable and enjoyable.

At the risk of placing a star in our own crown, it's very important to us to have all this information as up-to-date as possible. Some guidebooks make no attempt to deal with exact prices at all and are therefore sometimes put together a year before their actual sale and use. We try mightily not to do it that way.

Now, however, seems as good a time as any to say the obvious: prices change, airlines gain and lose routes, European rail and bus companies add or drop discount tickets and currency exchange rates are as volatile as the Zurich gold market. And neither we nor any other publisher of travel books can stop inflation and its effect on your trip budget.

Yet we sincerely hope that every bit of information here will make a real contribution to the planning and enjoyment of your trip. After almost three decades of foreign travel we are still looking for answers ourselves. But here are a few good ones we've found.

Planning your trip. It's nice to think you can step off a plane and watch Europe unfurl before your eyes like a pageant, but unfortunately it seldom happens that way. So take the time to lay out a general route to follow and then start a notebook or file folder for your trip. Cram it with information on the places you intend visiting. Clip from the travel columns of your local newspaper, magazines, tourist brochures and from any other sources of good information on the bistros, petrol prices, regional foods, museums, vineyards or whatever may interest you along the way.

Our trip notebooks always hold clippings from such diverse sources as *Gourmet* magazine, *Travel & Leisure,* the *New York Times, Los Angeles Times* and *London Observer, Travel/Holiday* and the colorful, informative and up-to-date travel writings of Horace Sutton, Stan Delaplane, Jerry Hulse, Joseph Wechsberg, Murray Brown, Kate Simon and whoever else writes sensibly, honestly and with perception about the places we're headed for.

Your library or bookstore is loaded with great books on travel, everything from James Michener's *Iberia* to the insight and perspective of Luigi Barzini's *The Italians* and Honor Tracy's reflections on Spain. As we said, Kate Simon's books bring a glow to any place she visits and the Time-Life *Foods of the World* cookbook series is just about the best set of "travel" books you'll find. They're absolutely crammed with the color, tempo, tradition, food and folkways of Europe, most of it in stunning color photography.

Who else can help? Almost every European country maintains one or more travel offices over here and they're staffed with professionals trained to give you general information or answer specific questions. You'll get invaluable help with a short letter or phone call. One good tip, however, is to be as specific in your requests as possible. If you're interested in France's Dordogne Valley, Provence, Burgundy or Loire chateaux, ask for brochures on those regions. Simply asking for all the information they have on France usually won't help much because it's impossible to send you fifty pounds of literature. We've included a page in the back that gives you their addresses. Use it. It's a marvelous travel tool.

European airlines and our own flag carriers have offices that are loaded with enthusiastic and knowledgeable people, plus great brochures for cities on their routes. A young woman at SAS once got us to New York, Lisbon, Madrid and Paris for an extra eight dollars or so on our basic Los Angeles-Copenhagen round-trip tickets. Pay them a visit if they're nearby and they will make a real contribution to your trip.

Packing. Telling someone what to pack is a little like telling your daughter what to wear to the prom. She will wear — and have the best time in — what she is comfortable with. We've traveled through the Greek isles twice wearing nothing but cotton denims and were the envy of every American we met, on shipboard or off. But we switch to our staple dark-blazer-and-slacks for him and what the fashion people call a "little drinking and praying dress" for me when we do the Vienna opera, Bolshoi or evening out in London. Take along a lightweight raincoat that doubles as a robe (for that dash down the hall) and let's assume that by now you know your weekly quota of underwear, stockings and the like. European stores sell soap, razor blades, shampoo, tooth paste, Kleenex, even cosmetics, so there's no need to pack along a footlocker of those either. It boils down to this: pack the sort of things you travel in at home, and take *only* luggage you can *carry personally* in comfort.

Our standard gear is one 21-inch suitcase per person, plus a spacious shoulder bag each. Two people can share a hanging suit/dress bag comfortably. This luggage mix will get you through three months of European travel dressed as appropriately as anyone you'll meet. And too much luggage will take the joy out of travel faster than anything we know.

What will it cost? This is the stickiest wicket of all because it's so hard to get a straight answer. There are even travel books that proclaim *"Wherever You Want on $20 a Day."* Fairy tales aside, Europe is expensive. How expensive is up to you. To help you we've worked out a formula over many years for the independent European traveler. It takes into consideration your style, which is to say what you enjoy and how much you'll pay to enjoy it. Call it whatever you like, but it goes like this:

Budgeting. *The total daily expenses of two people traveling together will be two-and-one-half times their double-room hotel rate.* This includes everything but inter-city transportation and gifts. Room, meals, museums, cabs, theater tickets, snacks, drinks, sightseeing tours — the lot — are covered by this formula. Keeping it in mind will help you decide which countries and cities you choose to visit, since a city's hotel prices and other costs tend to be on the same curve. Our formula might get out of line either way on a given day, but we think you'll find it pretty close to the mark at trip's end. *Voila!* Budgeting is simple. It's just a matter of never having to cash your last traveler's check!

Other planning tips. Get your hands on the best map of Europe you can find. Every year we set sail with another Hallwag *Europa* plus their city and country maps for the places we're visiting. Try your bookstore. These Swiss maps are perfect. With their city maps you can pick the general area of your hotel before arrival and they're worth their weight in gold once you're there.

Ask your bank for a supply of brand new one dollar bills. The new ones take very little wallet space and come in handy when you would rather not cash a $20 traveler's check into local currency for a small purchase just before leaving a country.

Make hotel reservations for the evening of your arrival in Europe as well as for the last night. You know exactly where you'll be and why start or finish a vacation looking for a place to sleep?

Give every consideration to late spring or September-October for your trip. Weather can be a bit unstable during the former, but fall in Europe is beautiful with prices to match.

Purchase, or purloin from your friendly supermarket, at least a dozen of those flimsy plastic vegetable bags. They're perfect for soiled or damp clothing and bits and pieces of other things, such as toiletries and film rolls, that tend to scatter throughout your luggage.

Take a break. If your trip will be a long one (a month or more) plan time for a three or four-day layover around mid-point. Then pick a smaller town or village that suits your fancy and relax from the heady pace. You won't regret it and your trip will certainly be more enjoyable. After all, travel should be recreation in its true sense of re-creating strength and lifting your spirits.

When you write for a reservation be sure to include an International Postal Coupon (available at post offices) for the hotel's reply. It works wonders. And when you're informed that there is a room available, send a check to cover the first night immediately.

Be sure that your traveler's checks or letter-of-credit is from an internationally known institution. American Express, Bankamerica, First National City, Thomas Cook and Barclays are just about it for checks and they are available across the country at other banks and savings and loans. A traveler's check on your friendly neighborhood bank is Confederate money in Italy.

Travel within Europe. This boils down to an economic choice, tempered somewhat by your own feelings about personal mobility as well as the type of itinerary you plan. The average cost of a small rental car in the *Ford Fiesta, Fiat 127* or *Volkswagen Rabbit* class is $218 per week with unlimited mileage, plus 15 percent average tax. Those figures are the norms for two car rental firms (*Hertz* and *Avis*) operating in the 23 countries we checked.

The same 23 countries had an average fuel cost of $2.25 per US gallon at that time. European gasoline is sold by the liter, which you multiply by 3.79 to arrive at the gallon cost. In Britain the Imperial gallon is 4.55 liters, 20% more than our gallon.

So having the car three weeks and averaging, say, 82 miles per day (see below) will cost you a total of $861.88. That's three weeks' car rental and tax ($752.10) plus fuel costs

($109.78) at 40 miles per gallon, no problem at all with the three economy models above.

Car rental rates. For current car rental rates in those countries you plan to visit, here are three toll-free telephone numbers to call: *Avis,* (800) 331-2112; *Hertz,* (800) 654-3001; *Budget,* (800) 527-0770. These companies, and of course others both here and abroad, usually have a seasonal-special rate based on advanced booking of perhaps two weeks. These specials can represent a considerable saving if your plans are made far enough in advance.

Don't push. If the 82 miles per day strikes you as too little, consider that it's a 21-day average for nine days of driving around a 1,723-mile loop from Paris through Munich, Salzburg, Vienna, Innsbruck, Geneva and Paris again to return the car. The other 12 days are spent sightseeing in these cities or in the towns and villages along the way.

It is also a sensible and comfortable pace, based on our own trip averages in driving the motorways and secondary roads of Europe every year.

Now split that $861.88 between two or three people in the car and you have a transportation cost per person within Europe, less taxi, bus or metro fares in big cities, where it's always smart to leave your car parked anyway.

Compare this figure with the $330 a 1983 *Eurailpass* will cost per person for 21 days of first-class train travel in 16 European countries. Now you are prepared to make a choice based on your own budget and itinerary.

Eurail versus you-drive. Both ways of travel have their advantages and drawbacks. Briefly, if you want to stop only in major European cities, with long distances in between, then take the *Eurailpass.* Car rental, driving time and fuel for a three-week itinerary through Amsterdam, Paris, Madrid, Rome, Vienna, Munich and Amsterdam again, a distance of more than 3,800 miles, would be foolhardy. Even if you allotted but two days in each city, you would spend an average 425 miles driving on each of the other nine days, a killing pace on European roads.

Eurailpass costs/information. For 1983 the *Eurailpass* (first-class) and *Eurail Youthpass* (under 26 years only) will cost you: $260, 330, 410, 560 and 680 for a 15-day, 21-day, 1-month, 2-month and 3-month *Eurailpass*; $290 for a 1-month *Eurail Youthpass*, $370 for 2-months. For further information and maps write to: Trains, Box M, Staten Island, NY 10305 or Eurailpass Distribution Center, Box 300, Station R, Montreal, Quebec H2S 3K9.

For more specific information on train travel in individual countries, write to their representatives. You will find a list of them in the latter pages of this book. Many of the individual country passes, such as the *Austria Ticket* or *Finnrailpass*, may be purchased through *German Federal Railroad* offices in this country. But remember, the *Eurailpass must* be purchased *before* your arrival in Europe.

Trans-Europ-Express (TEE). Since the early 1950s our memories of European trains have been almost all good, and some of the fondest are of *TEE* trains linking more than 130 larger cities. These all-first-class trains can reach speeds of 140 miles per hour and your *Eurailpass* (first-class) of course allows you to use them, although seats must be reserved and there's a moderate charge to be paid for this when booking a journey. *TEEs* are also all daytime trains, their high speeds usually getting you there before nightfall.

Eurailpass bargains. There are other ways of saving with *Eurailpass* if you don't mind a night train now and then. A crack express leaves Paris every evening at 11:15 p.m. and arrives in Munich the next morning at 9:33. A very comfortable *couchette* sleeper this year costs only $11 per person throughout the 16 *Eurailpass* countries, and on the Paris-Munich run it would save two traveling together about $20 for the night, based on the $43-plus they could expect to pay for a double room in either of these two cities.

Almost every *Eurail* country offers either free or substantially reduced tickets on the excellent *Europabus* network, lake steamers and domestic bus lines. The same is true for ferry service, including free passage between Ireland-France, Italy-Greece, Sweden-Finland and Germany-Denmark-Sweden. And, contrary to the major-city itinerary mentioned above, *Eurailpass* will take you to almost all towns of any size in 16 countries. Having used the *Eurailpass* on several occasions, we're convinced that it's the greatest thing to happen for European travelers since the end of World War II.

Other rail-bus passes. Nearly every country in Europe has some sort of rail or rail-bus pass of its own and these are described in the introductions to individual countries in the pages ahead. Almost all of them (*BritRail, France Vacances,* the Irish *Rambler* and Swiss *Holiday Card*, etc.) are bargains. Yet getting around in Europe is still very much a personal choice, one to be considered with your own budget and travel objectives in mind.

Once you're there. Be prepared for the occasional hotel that quotes room prices based upon full or half-pension. That's all meals or breakfast and one other. If you would rather not dine there, then insist on bed and breakfast only. The hotel's reaction will depend upon their room count for the night, but be adamant and you'll probably get what you want.

When writing for a reservation you will almost surely get one of the more expensive rooms unless you specifically ask for something modest. Keep this one in mind.

If you like to keep a fairly loose itinerary then one of the foolproof ways of avoiding both the above inconveniences is with the telephone. Long distance is not expensive in Europe and we always call ahead for reservations if we expect that a town will be crowded. If language is a problem have your present hotel desk make the call for you. Somehow they always convince the next stop that you don't want the presidential suite.

More hotel tips. Never hesitate to ask to see a hotel room before accepting. Acting interested will get you a better room and better service, or the opportunity to turn it down.

Select your hotel before nightfall if possible, preferably by late afternoon. You'll have a better idea of its neighborhood, available transportation and nearby restaurants.

The "bath or no bath" decision is up to you. We always decide based upon cost and how convenient a public bath is to the room. Most of these facilities are absolutely immaculate in Europe. And we never had a bathless hotel room without a washbasin with hot and cold running water.

Check a hotel's dining room, particularly its menu, if you expect to be there for mid-day or evening meals. It could save you disappointment later.

A Continental breakfast may be included in your room price, but a full, All-American breakfast will add appreciably to your bill. Except of course in England, Ireland, Holland and some Scandinavian countries where you'll stagger from the bounteous breakfast feast often included.

Always lock your luggage when leaving the room. In a couple of decades of European travel we've had only a few small things disappear, but it was always an inconvenience and always our own fault.

Don't be bashful. Ask your hotel desk for absolutely any assistance or advice you need during your stay. You'll be surprised at the good restaurants, difficult theater tickets, scarce rental cars and unusual sightseeing suggestions they come up with.

Settle your bill the evening before leaving. There are at least a half dozen reasons for this, all good.

Tipping is another very personal matter. If there is a service charge included on the bill, we go very light. But if a maid or porter has given special service or courtesies, we're just as gracious with the gratuities. There is more nonsense written about the obligatory percentages of European hotel and restaurant tipping than on any other subject we can think of. Tip what makes *you* feel comfortable, keeping in mind that European help never works for tips alone as it often does here.

Dining well on short dollars. We can think of nothing more debilitating to liver and spirit alike than a full-fledged gourmet tour of Europe. While we adore fine food and are awe-struck by chefs who have truly mastered its preparation, our one non-stop bout with pate, pressed duck and petits-fours left us limp after eight days on a New York-Genoa liner. If dining checks had been involved, it would have left us impecunious as well.

You can dine well *off* the three-star circuit in Europe by seeking out the small, colorful and usually less expensive places frequented by Europeans themselves. Food quality and portions are catered to the local taste and sense of values, which means you too will enjoy very good dining at very fair prices.

Keep your eye out for those places in the following countries and you'll be *shillings* ahead.

Austria and Germany: *Gastatte* is their word for restaurant. *Gasthof* and *gasthaus* are the country words, double as inns and are often more modest. *Bierstube* and *weinstube* serve some food but it wouldn't be correct to say they serve light food! Many hotels and restaurants have a second class dining room called the *schwemme* where prices are lower, but food is the same as that served under the chandeliers upstairs and we prefer them.

Belgium and France: It's their word and you'll find plenty of *restaurants,* almost all very good and it's really just a matter of price. *Auberge* is a small inn, often with overnight accommodations and not always modest, in city or countryside. *Bistro,* dining only, few tables and frequently a mom-and-pop affair with steady local customers. *Relais de campagne,* a relay or stage stop in the countryside that is sure to dazzle your palate. *Routier,* another roadside place that must satisfy a French truck driver and he knows his *escargot. Brasserie,* a bar with food and the better ones know that customers aren't there for a drink.

England, Scotland, Ireland: The pub is always a good stop for sturdy food at modest prices, some fairly elaborate, some bordering on grim. Other short-order places are not Britain's *forte*.

Greece: The *taverna* is every Greek's home-away-from-home. They're colorful, smoky and you always visit the kitchen to inspect the fare before ordering, like any sensible Greek. *Psistarya* is a very modest rotisserie at curbside or inside and the roasting lamb always simmers.

Italy: *Ristorante,* first cabin. *Trattoria,* family style, smaller and more fun. *Osteria,* neighborhood bar-restaurant for locals. *Tavola calda,* a "hot table" place that can range from stand-up to tables with flowers. *Rosticceria,* almost always stand-up. *Taverna,* small and usually picturesque. *Pizzeria,* you guess! *Locanda,* a country inn right off a travel poster.

Netherlands: The *broodjeswinkel* is a deli-like establishment that serves *broodjes,* simple hot or cold sandwiches that the Dutch devour all day. *Rijsttafel,* a "rice table" Indonesian restaurant with enough fiery food at modest prices to fill your eyes with tears and your table with little white plates. And don't miss those herring stands along the streets if your budget is tight.

Portugal: *Pousada* is comparable to the Spanish *parador* and also government-run as a showplace. *Estalagem,* a privately run inn or hotel, usually more expensive than a *pousada* and not always as good.

Spain: *Restaurante,* just what it says. *Parador,* government-run hotels in old castles, converted monasteries, convents or perhaps just built yesterday. Local food served by help in local costumes and they're awfully difficult to book overnight. Plan ahead! *Albergues,* country inns that range from very good to excellent. *Hosteria,* on the same order but less architectural overtones. *Meson, bodega, cantina* and *bar* are frequently modest or rustic and some serve *tapas,* the little five-to-eight goodies that get you through to the 10 or 11 p.m. evening meal. Miss the *tapas* hour and you miss Spain!

Scandinavia: You'll find variations of *smorbrod* shops (butter bread) throughout Scandinavia where marvelous open-face sandwiches are served. The Danes say *smorrebrod* and the Swedes *smorgas.* Denmark has its *polser* and *varm korv* street stands where you grab a quick hot dog, sausage or hamburger. The Danish *kros* are countryside inns, some with beds, noted for their traditional food and warm atmosphere.

Switzerland: Refer to France, Germany or Italy, depending upon which part of Switzerland you're in.

The list of Austrian *heurigen* (new wine houses) and *wurstl* stands, Bulgarian *mekena* (taverns) and Czech family style *pivarna* and *vinarna* (beer and wine houses) is endless. But the places above should keep your appetite and budget under control through your trip.

Try to read a restaurant's menu (many put them in the window) for prices before entering. The *prix fixe* meal is usually a real bargain. Sometimes called the "tourist menu," it can be imaginative and tasty, or downright dull. So check the day's offering, and look around at other diners, before signing up for this one.

Picnics are simple. We certainly should mention the joys of dining right out there in that *Sound of Music* scenery, and it's easier than you think. Just walk into a small market and collect a chub of salami, flute of fresh, sturdy bread, a chunk or two of cheese, small tin of pate, some grapes or other fruit, liter of wine and cans of super-rich fruit juices for the children. All you need now is a sharp knife and cork-screw, which you should already have or buy the first day. A picnic is the perfect mid-day break and you might even find local companions for a family style outing. We picnicked by a Russian lake once and ended up washing our car and several others with nearby Russians. Very few words but lots of laughs and a clean car for Leningrad.

Sightseeing. Giving advice on this is a little like the paragraph on packing. It's another "to each his own" subject. But one general rule has helped us and it will help you. If you know nothing about a large city, or you're overpowered by it all, don't hesitate to take a half-day *American Express* or other local tourist company's morning tour. It will highlight the city and give you numerous points of reference for later navigation on your own. Vienna, Madrid, Athens or Istanbul will slip into focus a lot faster on your first visit using this method.

Passport hotels and prices. Travelers usually move in twos so we have chosen to quote prices for double rooms only. Every effort has been made to give prices that reflect a fair and current *median* of *summer* rates for a double room with a private bath. If more than one price is given, the higher amount is for a more desirable room. Many of our hotels have rooms available without baths. These rooms will always be less expensive but, as noted before, will always have a washbasin with hot and cold running water.

Taxes and service, where not included, should average 15-20% during your trip. An extra bed placed in a double room will add about 30% to your bill, but single rooms may run from 70% to 100% of double room prices during high season.

Prices are given in dollars and please be aware that they will *vary with exchange fluctuations.* Some European currencies are very volatile and the dollar itself has been no Rock of Gibraltar recently, so *please, please* keep this in mind. And of course most travel guides make no effort to give exact hotel prices at all.

Please note that the number behind the boldface listing of the town is its postal code (in large cities it's behind the hotel's street address). The telephone prefix (in parentheses) need not be dialed if you are calling from within the town. If a street address is not given, the hotel either doesn't have one or there is no need for one because of the town or village's small size.

Other price factors. We *cannot* of course be responsible for the absolute accuracy of prices, since personal experience has shown that they may change at any moment and for a variety of reasons. Governments, when inflation strikes, are likely to approve blanket price increases or individual hotel category changes overnight, usually in late spring and impossible to predict. A holiday, trade fair, music festival or convention can play havoc with a city's hotel prices, even when they are supposedly controlled, and the peak tourist season in Paris, Venice, or any popular city can be a nightmare to the tired traveler arriving in the evening without reservations. The June-to-August tourist creates a supply-and-demand price situation that almost defies control, whether for rooms, meals, opera tickets or *bel canto* gondoliers!

Characteristics and location. We have tried to give you some idea of why each hotel is included in our guide. Perhaps the dining room is outstanding; the setting may be on a beach or lake; or perhaps because it's the best hotel value in a less well-known scenic spot or village that we think you will enjoy. In the latter case we either give the exact location or try to tell you something of its surroundings. In short, we want you to have some feeling for the place before your arrival.

Europe, big and small. We have always enjoyed our visits to Europe's large cities during the five years we lived there as well as on our frequent return trips. They are exhilarating, enlightening and overflowing with endless pleasures. Yet our fondest memories of Europe will always be of the Irish or Welsh farmhouse, the whitewashed inn on a Greek isle, the Cornwall fishing village or the small chalet hugging the top of an Austrian or Swiss mountain. And our hearts just sink at the thought we'll never visit every Tuscan hill town.

We hope this book helps you find the Europe we've found. And please let us know of any small hotels or inns that you feel we should check on for possible additions. Or any already here that you feel shouldn't be. Your letters have been an immense help during the past two decades, so please write to me directly at: Passport Publications; Box 24684; Los Angeles, CA 90024. We sincerely appreciate it.

And we also hope — sentiment aside — that this *Passport* and others in our series are your most convenient sources of useful information during your trip. Tuck us in your pocket or purse. . . we'll stay out of the way and try to earn our keep.

Bon Voyage!

Beverly Beyer

Landhaus Wegscheider / Salzburg

Austria

Here's the country that's rivaled only by Switzerland for spectacular mountain scenery, quiet lakes, charming alpine villages and cozy little chalets wearing a garland of geraniums at every turn in the road. Germany's Bavaria dips into central Austria, but the characteristic Bavarian costumes of *lederhosen* and *dirndls* are seen throughout the land. Vienna, once the capital of an Austro-Hungarian Empire of 40 million souls, now runs the affairs of but six million, which leaves plenty of time for drinking tea in the city's government offices. *Alt Wien* has become a terribly expensive city in the past five years, but it sparkles with an array of baroque architecture unmatched in Europe, lovely parks and gardens in the central city, the chestnut-tree-lined *Ringstrasse* describing the old town and ten months of opera, concerts and other musical events to do credit to a half-dozen capital cities. Vienna demands a few days from any serious traveler.

Vienna's summer temperatures hover in the low 60s and

70s, with December-March usually close enough to freezing for any snowbird. Fall and late spring can be glorious, but rain and raw weather make their appearances on any page of the calendar.

Austrian Airlines confines its routes to Europe, but you may reach Vienna from Canada by *Air Canada. Hertz, Avis, National, Inter-rent* and *Auto-Europe* are car hire firms in Austria, with a small car such as Ford's *Fiesta* or the VW *Polo* costing about $216 per week with unlimited mileage, plus a whopping 31% tax. Fuel, sold by the liter as it is in all of Europe, costs approximately $2.40 per US gallon for "super" at this time and you are urged to get an International Driver's License from your auto club before leaving.

Austria's railway system, like most in Europe, is marvelous and it honors *Eurailpass*, plus having its own *Austria Ticket* discount pass. A first-class *Austria Ticket* for 9 or 16 days costs approximately $140 and $200, second-class coach $105 and $150 for the same periods. A *Youth Ticket* for those under 26 is available for coach travel for 9 and 16 days at $70 and $95. Unlike *Eurailpass*, these tickets may be purchased at any Austrian Railways office after your arrival, or from German Federal Railroads offices in the US and Canada. Their exact cost depends upon the latest Austrian *schilling* exchange rate. A bus sytem links every hamlet in the country and cost is exactly the same as second-class rail.

The *schilling* is Austria's currency, broken into 100 *groschen*. At the present time a *schilling* is worth .055 or about 18 to the dollar. Banking hours are 8:00-12:30 and 1:30-3:30 Monday through Friday, 5:30 on Thursdays. Stores are open 8:30-5:30 Monday-Saturday. Electric voltage in Austria is 220 AC/50 cycles.

Austrian tables draw heavily from the old Austro-Hungarian Empire for staple dishes, which means a full measure of pork, veal and game, plus the ever-present potato. The veal *schnitzel* is Austria's national dish and you'll find it prepared in endless dozens of ways, all enjoyable. Wines, mostly white, are usually on the sweet side and most restaurants have an *offen wein* of red and white. Nobody makes better pastry than the Austrians, as a trip to Vienna's *Demel's* at tea time will prove beyond any doubt. Sensible tips are three to five percent as a service charge is always included in your bill.

Austria's Vorarlberg and Arlberg to the west offer spectacular mountain scenery and skiing, but the alpine passes into Italy are just as breathtaking and the Salzkammergut lake region near Salzburg can't be missed. While Innsbruck, Salzburg and many of the country's internationally known resorts have become as expensive as Vienna, dining and lodging values abound in the villages and countryside if your eyes are sharp. We still rate the country-at-large as medium-priced, with budget accommodations and food for the less demanding.

Hotels & Inns

Bad Aussee, A-8990 Steiermark

Haus Fasching | Double with bath *$28*
c/o Johanna Koeberl | Telephone (06152)2170

Small but comfortable pension in Steiermark's scenic northwest lake region. Only three private baths, so write or call ahead.

Bad Ischl, A-4820 Oberosterreich (Salzkammergut)

Schenner | Double with bath *$34*
Bad Ischl 4820 | Telephone (06132)2327

A rustic charming inn right in the center of this spa town of Austria's lake region. Loaded with *gemutlichkeit* throughout.

Durnstein, A-3601 Niederosterreich

Gasthof Blondel
c/o Johann Schendl

Double with bath *$35*
Telephone (02711)253

Excellent food, Wachau wine in picture-perfect Danube village 40 miles west of Vienna, a traditional Sunday outing for Viennese.

Feldkirch, A-6911 Vorarlberg

Alpenrose
Rosengasse 6

Double with bath *$36*
Telephone (05522)22175

In 20 years we've never failed to receive a hearty Austrian welcome at this sparkling inn at center of medieval town.

Fieberbrunn, A-6391 Tirol

Gasthof Auwirt

Double with bath *$27*
Telephone (05354)6238

Another reader favorite for years, probably for the authentic Tirolean food from its kitchen. Not far east of Kitzbuhel.

Gmunden, A-4810 Oberosterreich (Salzkammergut)

Gasthof Steinmauer
Edge of lake

Double with bath *$28*
Telephone (07612)4239

You'll enjoy the fresh fish filets served at tables outside overlooking lake. Rather spartan and away from town center.

Gasthof Goldner Hirsch
Town center

Double with bath *$27*
Telephone (07612)4386

Another cozy one with equally good Austrian food. Take traditional Traunsee cruise on ancient steamer. A favorite fall stop with us.

Graz, A-3601 Steiermark

Kirchenwirt
A-8044 Mariatrost

Double with bath *$35*
Telephone (03122)391112

Every possible amenity, including a sauna, at this medium-sized hotel in medieval city, now unfortunately a manufacturing center.

Hallstatt, A-4830 Oberosterreich

Gasthof Zauner   Double with bath *$25*
On market square   Telephone (06134)246

Charming chalet in one of the Salzkammergut's most fetching villages. Superior food and but a short walk down to lake.

Heiligenblut, A-9844 Karnten

Hotel Post   Double with bath *$36*
Main square   Telephone (04824)2245

Our favorite stop on Grossglockner Pass, one of Europe's most scenic, down into Italy. Views from hotel are stunning.

Innsbruck, A-6020 Tirol

Schwarzer Adler   Double with bath *$40-55*
Kaiserjagerstrasse 2   Telephone (05222)27109

So Tirolean you won't believe it, with vaulted ceilings, typical *Stuben,* wine cellar and some of the best food in all Innsbruck.

Weisses Kreutz   Double with bath *$35-45*
Herzog-Friedrichstrasse 31   Telephone (05222)1890

A notch below but every bit as imposing as *Schwarzer Adler*, 500 years old, perfect location and Mozart praised its atmosphere.

Igls, A-6080 Tirol

Pension Panarama
                                   Double with bath *$28*
                                   Telephone (05222)77382

Readers have written warmly of the friendly welcome and good food here for more than 20 years. Village high above Innsbruck.

Kitzbuhel, A-6370 Tirol

Tennerhof
                                   Double with bath *$45-65*
                                   Telephone (05356)3181

In a parklike setting on the sunny side of the village and this has to be Kitzbuhel's finest. Marvelous food, sauna, solarium.

Christophorus   Double with bath *$32*
                               Telephone (05356)2784

Breakfast only served at this longtime favorite, but you can't beat these prices in ever-jumping Kitzbuhel. Winters always higher.

Hotel Tyrol   Double room/full pension *$47*
                               Telephone (0536)2468

Some smaller places still insist on full-pension, but it's usually a huge bargain and food always very typical here.

Lech, A-6764 Voralberg

Haus Widderstein   Double with bath *$33*
c/o Josef Jochum   Telephone (05583)452

Only 12 rooms but all with bath and readers have been happy here for decades. More good dining. Prices skyrocket in mid-winter.

Mariazell, A-8630 Steiermark

Goldene Krone   Double with bath *$32*
c/o Christine Moser   Telephone (02727)2583

A perfect charmer of a village in summer or winter and not far from Vienna. We've enjoyed this sparkling hotel since the 50s.

Saalbach, A-5753 Salzburg

Sonne   Double with bath *$38*
                               Telephone (06586)7202

Large chalet in this popular ski resort that continues to grow. Full pension available, which includes sturdy soups daily.

Salzburg, A-5020

Landhaus Wegscheider   Double with bath *$35*
Thumeggerstrasse 4   Telephone (06222)41764

Frau Wegscheider is a near saint who has looked after readers' needs since 50s. Lots of fruit trees in garden, on edge of busy city.

Elefant   Double with bath *$46*
Sigmund-Haffnergasse 4   Telephone (06222)43409
Practically a landmark on a narrow street at dead center of
town. An inn since 13th-century. Fine regional dining at
Stiftskeller.

St. Anton, A-6580 Arlberg

Haus Muir   Double (no baths) *$29*
c/o Albert Muir   Telephone (05446)2300
Small, family run, the sort of place you hope to find every
night. St. Anton perfect town for skiing Zurs, Lech, St.
Christoph.

Mooserkreuz   Double with bath *$42-55*
West of village   Telephone (05446)2230
Just outside town on St. Christoph Road and this chalet's
rates include indoor swimming pool, sauna, hotel bus service.

Fremdenhiem Flunger   Double (no baths) *$24*
                                        Telephone (05446)2597
A small neat place with geranium boxes on the balconies,
which your room will probably have. A twin of *Haus Muir*
nearby.

St. Wolfgang, A-5360 Oberosterreich (Salzkammergut)

Gasthaus Dr. Leifer   Double with bath *$33-41*
Outside town on lake   Telephone (06138)800
One of St. Wolfgang's prettiest, set in a garden at lakeshore
with private beach. Take old steamer to St. Gilgen at lake's
end.

White Horse Inn   Double with bath *$50-64*
Center of town   Telephone (06138)306
A stay at the *Weisses Rossl* is almost a must for anyone visiting Austria's Salzkammergut. Right on lake and enchanting
throughout.

Schruns, A-6780 Voralberg

Taube

Double with bath *$32-45*
Telephone (05556)2384

Ernest Hemingway returned often to Schruns and always stayed at the *Taube*, drawn there by the friendly staff and marvelous food.

Seefeld, A-6100 Tirol

Stern

Double with bath *$44-48*
Telephone (05212) 2235

Very good value and located on beautiful Innsbruck-Garmisch road above lovely Inns Valley. Pension prices particularly reasonable.

Tauplitzalm, A-8982 Steiermark

Gasthof Alpenrose

Double with bath *$32-38*
Telephone (03688)320

Would you believe a 2½ mile chairlift, one of the world's longest, to this glorious resort? *Alpenrose* has only half-pension plan.

Velden, A-9220 Karnten

Carinthia
On lake

Double with bath *$38-48*
Telephone (04274)2171

A holiday on Worthersee is as traditional with Austrians as *lederhosen* and the *Carinthia* one of the finest hotels on lake.

Villach, A-9500 Karnten

Post
Hauptplatz 26

Double with bath *$45-50*
Telephone (04242)26101

Villach, in heart of Corinthian Alps near Italian border, is good Vienna-Venice stop. *Hotel Post* has charmed us more than once.

Vienna

Kaerntnerhof
1010 Grashofgasse 4

Double with bath *$50-56*
Telephone (0222)521923

Our hometown for two years and every return means a stay at this fine hotel with perfect location behind St. Stephens Cathedral.

Pension Pertschy
1010 Habsburgergasse 5

Double with bath *$38*
Telephone (0222)523867

Very modest but best location in Vienna within walking distance of opera house, palace, St. Stephens, Graben and Kaerntnerstrasse.

Pension Christina
1010 Hafnersteig 7

Double with bath *$40*
Telephone (0222)632961

A neat little place, owned by the Pertschy people above, behind St. Stephens and near the Danube Canal. Excellent value, location.

King of Hungary
1010 Schulerstrasse 10

Double with bath *$64-72*
Telephone (0222)526520

After a recent facelift this one will whisk you back to the old Austro-Hungarian empire immediately. So traditional it hurts.

Pension Zenz
1090 Alserstrasse 21

Double with bath *$32-36*
Telephone (0222)425268

Very simple, modest and neat place near the University of Vienna and not far from *Volksoper*. Visiting professors love it dearly.

Zell am Zee, A-5700 Salzburg

Alte Post
Town center

Double with bath *$36*
Telephone (06542)2422

Post hotels in Austria and Germany always a local landmark and this one no exception. All meals plus a full pension plan.

Pension Schoenblick   Double with bath *$32*
Just outside town   Telephone (06542)7400

Every room with bath in this excellent pension a notch above the normal. We've been sending summer-winter guests here for years.

Vieux Chateau / La Roche-en-Ardenne

Belgium

Belgium is a small country with but 40 miles of coastline on the English Channel. Its character, cuisine and culture draw heavily on neighboring countries, yet it manages to retain a flavor and feeling all its own. The two major Belgian languages are really dialects of other tongues, Flemish-Dutch to the north and French to the south. You will find windmills and wooden shoes north of Brussels, and the lovely Ardennes forest is shared with France and Luxembourg in its southeast corner. With no predominant architectural style, no "national" dish recognizable on the menus of Europe and the 12,000 square miles of countryside predominantly flat, one might come to the conclusion that it could be bypassed for other, more "exotic" countries in Europe. To do so would be the traveler's loss.

For one thing, Belgium is one of the true art centers of Europe, particularly the Flanders cities of Ypres, Ghent and Bruges with its fine medieval buildings set off by the city's famous canals. The lode of paintings here by Rubens, Breughel, Van Dyck, Van Gogh and assorted other Flemish and Dutch masters defies belief. The Ardennes region remains one of the Continent's undiscovered joys, a bucolic wonderland of tumbling streams, dense forests and charming villages just waiting for the visitor sensible enough to spend a few relaxing days in one of its inviting old inns.

The Belgian airline *Sabena* and *Capitol* will fly you there from the US; *Air Canada* and *Sabena* from Canada. *Avis* and *Hertz* will rent you a *Fiat 127, Renault 5* or *Volkswagen Polo* for about $175 per week unlimited mileage, plus 25% tax. Fuel for it will cost you a little more than $2.50 a gallon.

Belgian railways of course accept the *Eurailpass* and also have discounts and excursions of their own. For getting off the beaten path you may need to take a bus, which are run by the nation's railway system and are relatively inexpensive. Direct your questions on discount rail and bus tickets to the country's railway office in New York, listed in the last pages of this book.

The Belgian *franc* is currency and it's split into 100 *centimes*. Right now the *franc* is worth .02 US or 50 to the dollar. Bank hours are 9:00-3:30, five days, with shops open from 9:00-6:00, six days. Voltage for most of Belgium is 220. Summer weather is in the 60s and 70s, winters almost always in the 30s.

One never thinks of a Belgian cuisine, as we have noted, but it is as imaginative and delectable as you are likely to find in Europe. And, just as in France, it ranges from the *haute cuisine* of elegant restaurants to the bracing dishes of peasant cookery. Eels are a passion in the north and they are quite good when cooked amid the complex flavor of a half-dozen herbs. The yearly fall appearance of mussels approaches a national holiday and they too are likely to convert non-*moule* lovers at one sitting.

With only 40 miles of coastline it is amazing the role seafood plays in Belgian dining, but count your blessings and enjoy every shrimp, oyster and Ostend sole placed before you. Ardennes ham is famous throughout the world and the wild boar and other game of that region will delight the most demanding diner. Belgian sausage is as good as you will find, rabbit and chicken are prepared as only the French and Belgians can and the delicate endive appears in soups, stews or stuffed with meat on just about every menu. Belgians, having no vineyards, drink beer like the Germans and it is excellent.

Alas, the good life in Belgium does not come all that cheap. Plan on moderate-to-expensive dining prices in small towns and villages, a good bit more in Brussels and other large cities.

Hotels & Inns

Antwerp, 2030 Antwerpen

Antwerp Docks   Double with bath *$42*
Nooderlaan 100   Telephone (031)411850

Just outside the central city and a favorite with our readers for many years. Excellent Oostende sole in restaurant here.

Assesse, 5330 Namur

La Truite d'Argent   Double with bath *$32-36*
Chaussee de Marche 89   Telephone (083)655444

Only seven rooms so book or call ahead as The Silver Trout is noted for its magnificent regional food and country setting.

Bastogne, 6650 Luxembourg (Ardennes)

Borges	Double with bath *$32-34*
Place Mac Auliffe 11	Telephone (062)211100

A small charmer in this historic town at the heart of the Ardennes Forest. Dining room will serve you region's famous ham.

Bouillon, 6830 Luxembourg (Ardennes)

Aux Armes de Bouillon	Double with bath *$36-38*
Rue de la Station 9	Telephone (061)466079

An older rustic style hotel in this delightful town, again in the Ardennes. Outstanding dining room and cheerful sidewalk cafe.

Brugge, 8000 West-Vlaanderen

De Barge	Double with bath *$28*
Komvest 41A	Telephone (050)331150

Just what it says, an old barge situated on a colorful canal of Brugge. Friendliest staff, Flemish food, only 11 rooms at this neat inn.

Central	Double with bath *$26-28*
Markt 30	Telephone (050)331805

Breakfast only at this older hotel right on the colorful market square of this fascinating city. Lots of fine budget dining nearby.

Pannenhuis	Double with bath *$38-45*
Zandstraat 2 8200	Telephone (050)311907

Splurge a bit at this old estate gone modern with a reputation among locals for outstanding food. Half-mile from town center.

Brussels, 1000 Brabant

Barry	Double with bath *$36-38*
Place Anneesens 25	Telephone (02)5113247

On a small square near town center with 16 neat doubles and

a bright little breakfast room with fresh flowers on the tables.

Grand Cloche   Double with bath *$32-34*
10 Place Rouppe   Telephone (02)5110956

Another neat but modest small one near the central city. You'll find excellent restaurants along Rue Bouchers near Grand Place.

Auberge Saint-Michel   Double with bath *$36-44*
Grand Place 15   Telephone (02)5110956

Probably the most stunning location in town, right on one of Europe's most beautiful and historic squares. Very few rooms.

Queen Anne   Double with bath *$42-48*
Blvd. Emile Jacqmain 110   Telephone (02)2171600

Not our usual type hotel, but they have 60 sparkling modern rooms, a small bar and the location is good. No dining.

Couvin, 6400 Namur

La Sapiniere   Double with bath *$34*
Rue Pied de Montagne 55   Telephone (060)344381

A mile outside this fetching town and known far and wide for its treatment of Ardennes regional food. Only 10 rooms, so call first.

Eupen, 4700 Liege

Hostellerie Chapeau Rouge   Double with bath *$34*
Aachenerstrasse 38   Telephone (087)55211

A stately old mansion in parklike setting and anyone would walk miles just to dine here. Ten rooms only, each with bath.

Hamoir, 4180 Liege (Ardennes)

Hostellerie de la Post   Double with bath *$26-28*
Rue du Pont 32   Telephone (086)388324

An old posting stop with six rooms and five baths and again the accent is on dining. Seafood supreme plus local wild boar.

Herbeumont, 6803 Luxembourg (Ardennes)

La Chatelaine
Double with bath *$35-38*
Grand Place 127
Telephone (061)411422

Large for a typical inn, with 36 rooms, most with private baths. Dining terrace where you may order your crayfish seven ways!

Hamois, 5360 Namur

Chateau de Pickeim
Double with bath *$34-38*
Route de Liege 136
Telephone (083)611274
(near Havelange)

This chateau looks more like a castle with 20 rooms beneath its twin towers. Trout, crayfish and frog legs a specialty of the chateau's kitchen. *Alors!*

Jalhay, 4804 Liege

La Couronne
Double with bath *$28-32*
Place 49
Telephone (087)647055

La Couronne stakes its reputation on the kitchen as there are only 15 rooms, one with private bath. Try *cassolette d'escargots*.

La Roche en Ardenne, 6980 Luxembourg

Vieux Chateau
Double with bath *$36-40*
Pesse rue 6
Telephone (084)411327

Our favorite small hotel in all Belgium, thanks to the Linchet family's total concern for their guests' well-being. Dishes from the extensive menu would grace any table in Brussels or Paris and La Roche shouldn't be missed by any Ardennes visitor.

Liege, 4000

Le Cygne d'Argent
Double with bath *$38-40*
Rue Beeckman 49
Telephone (041)237001

A country style inn at the heart of this bustling city on the Meuse River. Kitchen leans heavily and well on freshwater fish from it and other local rivers and streams.

Malmedy, 4890 Liege

Au Saint Esprit   Double with bath *$30-34*
Rue Jules Steinboch 17   Telephone (080)773314

Old fashioned hotel near center of this small town with half-dozen rooms. The kitchen will grill your lobster perfectly.

Stoument, 4984 Liege

Les Sept Collines   Double with bath *$32*
Route de l'Ambleve 89   Telephone (080)785984

Another typical roadside inn with marvelous view of the Ambleve Valley countryside. Lots of fowl dishes; try duck with raspberries!

Tokajik / Novy Smokovec

Czechoslovakia

This small nation of 15 million is one of Europe's youngest, having been carved from the richest industrial part of the old Austro-Hungarian Empire in the twilight of World War I. Bohemia, Moravia, Silesia, Ruthenia... Czech, Slovak, parts of regions and peoples were hammered into a new nation that was to show Central Europe and the world how democracy worked. Alas, on the eve of WWII the dismemberment of Czechoslovakia began as she lost one third of her people and territory to Germany, Poland and Hungary. After the war she disappeared behind the Iron Curtain as the Socialist Republic of Czechoslovakia.

But life goes on, with or without external guidance, and today the provinces of Bohemia, Moravia and Slovakia function as best they can, welcoming their visitors with a reasonable enough version of *la vie boheme*. What they lack in creature comforts is made up for in scenery, such hospitality as they can offer and a genuine fondness for anything and anybody from west of their borders.

Travel to Czechoslovakia is handled exclusively through *Cedok*, the national travel office, or one of its affiliated travel agencies in the US, Canada and abroad. *Cedok* has an office in New York and many European capitals, but unfortunately not in Canada. It's almost a must to get in touch with one of *Cedok's* affiliated agencies (ask *Cedok,* New York (212) 689-9720 for the one nearest your home) as a visa is necessary for travel there and they aren't issued at border points. There is also the matter of a minimum expenditure per person per day in the country ($15 each for adults at this writing, half that for children) and details for purchasing such vouchers *before* you enter the country are available from *Cedok*.

CSA, the Czech national airline, will fly you direct to Prague from New York and Montreal. Express trains between larger cities are very near Continental standards, with locals falling off a bit. They don't honor *Eurailpass* and have none of their own, so plan on spending about 45 *koruna*, around $4.81, for the first 100 kilometers of first-class rail travel, $3.50 second-class. Fares drop off per km. for longer trips and bus travel costs a little less than second-class rail.

Cedok offices in New York, Prague and other Czech cities offer all-inclusive bus tours throughout the country and they're excellent.

The *koruna (Kcs.)* is of course Czech currency, divided into 100 *halir*, and the official tourist exchange rate is now 10.25 *Kcs.* to the dollar. *Pragocar* and *Avis* are rental firms and a *VW Polo (Rabbit)* will cost you about $250 per week with unlimited mileage, plus 15% tax. Fuel is 9.50 *Kcs.* per liter or $3.51 per US gallon.

Banking hours are 8:00-4:00, five days and stores are generally open 9:00-6:00 six days. Voltage is 220.

Czech food is Central-European-heavy, without Hungarian

or Balkan spiciness, which means lots of pork, sauerkraut and *knedliky* bread dumplings, hearty stews with noodles, equally hearty sausages, goose, goulash, thick soups, sturdy breads and fine pastry. Germans brew great beer but Czechs brew the world's greatest, *Pilsner Urquell*, pure cream in a glass. Try a *pivarna* (beer garden) or *vinarna* (wine garden) for no-nonsense food, plus a visit to *U Fleku* brewery in Prague, a fixture since 1499. Czech wines also go very well with all this fare.

Czechs have been hotel poor for three decades now, but *Cedok's* chain of 220 *Interhotels* and other accommodations span the country and they're good, including those in the scenic High and Low Tatra mountains. Lodging prices, considering they include half-pension (breakfast plus another meal), and dining costs are both in the medium range, with budget food and drink available in the beer halls and wine gardens we mentioned.

Hotels & Inns
(All prices include breakfast and lunch or dinner)

Babylon, West Bohemia

Magda
345 31 Babylon

Double with bath *$33*
Telephone 321

This one is so old fashioned you won't believe it. Near the West German border. Reception desk in nearby *Hotel Praha*.

Bratislava, West Slovakia

Krym
801 00 Bratislava,
Safarikovo nam 6

Double with bath *$50*
Telephone 55471

A real study in Czechoslovakian baroque near the Old Danube Bridge. City close to Austrian border, short drive from Vienna.

Brno, South Moravia

Slovan
662 04 Brno/Lidicka 23

Double with bath *$60*
Telephone 54111

Right in the center of the country's second largest city and has usual amenities of restaurant, cafe, bar and wine cellar.

Jihlava, South Moravia

Jihlava Grand
58601 Jihlava, Husova 1

Double with bath *$39*
Telephone 23541

A good example of the city's baroque architecture with 34 rooms. Spend evenings in its *horacka rychta,* typical mountain bar.

Karlsbad *(Karlovy Vary),* West Bohemia

Central
36082 Karlovy Vary,
Leninovo nam 17

Double with bath *$38*
Telephone 25101

A medium-sized, comfortable place in one of world's most famous spas. Like most *Cedok* hotels, has currency exchange desk.

Luhacovice, South Moravia/Wallachia

Alexandria
76326 Luhacovice

Double with bath *$58*
Telephone 3311

Another delightful study in Czech architecture at the center of this spa town, also noted for folk art, costumes, dances.

Marianbad, (Marianski Lazne) West Bohemia

Corso
35301 Marianski Lazne,
tr. Odboraru 61

Double with bath *$40*
Telephone 3091

A 19th-century hotel, small, on the outskirts of Czechoslovakia's most popular spa. Veal a kitchen specialty, attractive winecellar.

Novy Smokovec, High Tatras

Tokajik
06201 Novy Smokovec

Double with bath *$48*
Telephone 2612

Handsome contemporary resort hotel in the country's favorite playground. Kitchen turns out game and fish from the region.

Pilsen, West Bohemia

Slovan
30520 Pilzen,
Smetanovy sady 1

Double with bath *$40*
Telephone 32238

Another 19th-century "grand" hotel in rather grim city. But *Pilsner Urquell* beer world's finest. Dining room puts it in their goulash.

Podbrezova, Low Tatras

Kosodrevina
97681 Podbrezoua,
Okres Banska Bystrica

Double with bath *$48*
Telephone 95105/Brezno

Sparkling modern resort hotel in beautiful Low Tatra mountains of central Czechoslovakia. Ski lift stops at hotel's front door.

Prague

Pariz
11000 Praha 1,
U Obecniho domu 1

Double with bath *$56*
Telephone 67551

A perfect example of Prague's baroque architecture on the north bank of Vlava River; both give city much of its character.

Flora
13000 Praha 3,
Vinohradska 121

Double with bath *$56*
Telephone 67551

Right at the center of Prague's old town with pre-Hapsburg furnishings and dining room noted for Moravian/German dishes.

Tatranska Lomnica, High Tatras

Lomnica

05960 Tatranska Lomnica

Double with bath *$44*

Telephone 967251

Cozy resort hotel at top of High Tatras on eastern Polish border. Slovak food, tap wine and gypsy music in lively cellar tavern.

Falsled Kro / Millinge

Denmark

Denmark is everyone's toyland, a tiny and very tidy country of islands filling the straits between Sweden and its own Jutland peninsula. It's about half the size of Maine with around five million Danes leading their own version of the good life: hard work followed by a free-wheeling lifestyle when business affairs are finished for the day. To-each-his-own is as good a description of the Danish attitude as you will find, with bars open practically around the clock and a very informal, loose or healthy attitude toward sex, depending upon the visitor's point-of-view.

All this adds up to some of the friendliest, happiest and most hospitable people in Europe, nearly all of whom speak perfect English.

The *krone*, divided into 100 ore, is Danish currency and it is currently worth about 11 cents US or 9 to the dollar. Banks are open from 10:00-4:00, five days, 6:00 p.m. on Thursdays, and closed Saturdays. Stores are usually open 9:00-5:30, later on Friday, and close Saturday for two hours at noon. Voltage in Denmark is 220. Summer temperatures are in the high 50s and 60s, winters in the 30s.

Danes love to eat and everywhere you will see their food displayed in colorful tiers, here a window banked with pastries in a *konditori*, next door a sandwich shop brimming with innumerable types of *smorrebrod*, those impossible-to-pass-up open-faced sandwiches. "Butter bread" is always the base, but anything from the garden, sea, butcher shop, dairy or orchard can be piled on top, and a restaurant in Copenhagen once boasted 500 varieties.

Frikadeller, ground veal and pork patties traditionally served with pickled beets and boiled potatoes, comes close to being the Danish national dish. Denmark's economy was almost totally agricultural not too long ago, so you will still find plenty of beef, veal, pork and fowl on menus, not to mention enough seafood to satisfy anyone. Tiny shrimp the size of a fingertip are towered on sandwiches and salads by the hundreds and herring, cooked or pickled, is a staple.

Roast loin of pork stuffed tight with prunes and apples is a festive dish and Danish ham is sought all over Europe. With plenty of dairy products at their command, the Danes rank very near the French and Swiss in turning out great cheeses. Try their version of Camembert, Brie, St. Paulin, Port-Salut, Blue and the nutty, caraway-laced Tybo from Jutland. Formidable indeed.

All this good life, Danish style, has become much more affordable for its visitors recently as prices have come more in line with those of its southern neighbors. On a recent Danish trip we found costs steadily approaching moderate, with of course plenty of expensive hotels and restaurants for those with richer tastes.

For total immersion into Danish life, keep your eyes peeled for the *kros* or countryside inns with their traditional food and cozy atmosphere. Mission hotels, *missionshotellets*, are modest, spotless lodgings throughout the country where your dollar will stretch as far as possible today in expensive Scandinavia.

SAS, Icelandic, Northwest Orient and *Finnair* airlines will fly you to Copenhagen from the US, *SAS* and *Air Canada* from Canada. *Avis, Hertz, Europcar* and *Pitzner Auto* are four of the larger rental firms and a Ford *Fiesta* will cost you about $150 per week unlimited mileage, plus a hefty 22% tax. Super fuel goes for about $2.75 a US gallon at this time, and driving in Denmark is a delight.

DSB, the Danish State Railways, honors *Eurailpass* and also participates in the *Nordturist Med Tag* Scandinavian tourist ticket plan with Sweden, Norway and Finland. You get 21 days of first or second-class rail travel in these countries for $227 or $151, children half that. A full month will cost you $285 first-class, $189 second, and tickets are availble at most stations throughout Europe. An excellent bus network services the smaller towns of Denmark.

Hotels & Inns

Aalborg, DK 9000

| Missionshotellet Ansgar | Double with bath *$32* |
| Prinsensgade 14 | Telephone (08)133733 |

Missionhotels throughout Denmark are always a good value but some serve nothing stronger than beer in dining rooms. Pity.

Ans, DK 8643

| Kongensbro Kro | Double with bath *$36* |
| Gl. Kongevej 77 | Telephone (06)870177 |

This riverside wonder of burnished wood, roaring hearths

and outstanding food is perfect example of Denmark's lovely *kros.*

Arhus, DK 8000

| Ansgar Missions Hotel | Double with bath *$38-40* |
| DK 8100, Banegardsplads 14 | Telephone (06)124122 |

Rather large for our book but the location is good in this Jutland city noted for contemporary architecture plus delightful Old Town.

Bogense, DK 5400

| Bogense Hotel | Double with bath *$26* |
| Adelgade 56 | Telephone (09)811108 |

Back to small ones with this 20-room inn with small garden and short walk to sea, where water is too cold for most mortals.

Copenhagen

Vestersohus	Double with bath *$54-60*
Vestersogade 58	Telephone (01)113870
DK 1601 Copenhagen V	

A remarkable recent discovery for us was *Vestersohus*, newly purchased and renovated into what is surely the city's most captivating small hotel. It overlooks a little canal near city center, guests gather in the rooftop rose garden in the evening to chat, enormous breakfasts feature jams made by the owner's wife and a double with breakfasts is yours for very reasonable Copenhagen prices. We fell in love with it.

Triton	Double with bath *$58-62*
Helgolandsgade 7	Telephone (01)230910
DK 1653 Copenhagen V	

Helgolandsgade is Copenhagen's "Sleeping Street," with a clutch of good little hotels all in a row, the main railway station just around the corner and within walking distance of Town Hall Square, Tivoli Gardens and airline bus stop station. *Triton* is very efficient study in Danish modern with rooms a bit on the small side.

Westend   Double with bath *$58*
Helgolandsgade 3   Telephone (01)314801
DK 1653 Copenhagen V

Another sparkling and efficient hotel with the same good location. A large Danish breakfast, which comes with room price at all Helgolandsgade places listed here, is the only meal served. Most rooms have small refrigerators and there are less expensive accommodations without private baths.

Hebron   Double with bath *$52*
Helgolandsgade 4   Telephone (01)316906
DK 1653 Copenhagen V

The same bounteous breakfasts of eggs, fresh baked bread, cheese, coffee and on and on. Near all of these hotels on Helgolandsgade you will find the *Froken Gelins Kaelder*, a pretty little cellar restaurant at No. 8 where you will dine very well indeed for very few *krone*.

Esbjerg, DK 6700

Kors Kroen   Double with bath *$26-29*
Skads Hovedvej 116   Telephone (05)120059

A marvelous stop for anyone driving Jutland's southwest coast. Small, as a *kro* should be, fine North Sea fish in dining room.

Fredensborg, DK 3480

Store Kro   Double with bath *$52-55*
Slotsgade 6   Telephone (02)280047

The King of Denmark himself built this *kro* in the early 18th century near Fredensborg Castle, not far from Hamlet's at Helsingor.

Hovborg, DK6682

Hovborg Kro   Double with bath *$38-44*
Holmeavej 2   Telephone (05)396033

Central Jutland is the location of this thatched-roof inn with beamed ceilings, fine Danish cooking. Built in early 19th century.

Kvistgard, DK 3490

Marianelund Kro
DK 3490 Kvistgard

Double with bath *$50*
Telephone (03)239064

When an inn is 460 years old is has the right to take on a fine patina of age. This one, snuggled in woods south of Helsingor, has.

Millinge, DK 5642

Falsled Kro
DK 5642 Falsled

Double with bath *$57*
Telephone (09)681111

We think this is probably the most attractive *kro* in Denmark; magnificent furnishings, exquisite food, glorious setting.

Steensgaard Herregardspension
Steengard 4
DK 5642 Millinge

Double with bath *$60-70*
Telephone (09)619490

Regal is hardly strong enough to describe this 700-year-old manor house set in a huge estate. Prepare to be overwhelmed by it all!

Mogel Tonder, DK 6270

Schackenborg Slotskro
Slotsgaden 42
DK 6270 Tondor

Double with bath *$24-28*
Telephone (04)778383

Modest as *kros* go, but you'll question that when confronted by the Herculean *smorrebrod* in fetching dining room. 350 years old.

Naestved, DK 4700

Menstrup Kro
DK 4700 Menstrup

Double with bath *$32*
Telephone (03)743003

Young for a *kro,* only about 200 years, but a perfect overnight stop for anyone arriving via ferry to Sealand from Germany.

Mogenstrup Kro
Praesto Landevej
(outside Naestved)

Double with bath *$38-40*
Telephone (03)761130

Forty rooms and all the ambiance, paneled walls, friendliness and fine dining you would expect. On Baltic 16 miles from Naestved.

Odense, DK 5000

Motel Odense   Double with bath *$35-38*
Hunderupgade 2   Telephone (09)114213

An old converted farmhouse on the Isle of Fyn between Sealand and Jutland. Scandinavian motels often have good dining rooms.

Ribe, DK 6760

Weis Stue   Double (no private baths) *$26*
Torvel 2   Telephone (05)420700

A 16th-century inn just off the west coast of southern Jutland in one of Denmark's most charming medieval towns. A little gem.

Skanderborg, DK 8660

Skanderborghus   Double with bath *$34-38*
Dyrehaven   Telephone (06)520955

Beautiful lakeside setting a few miles south of Arhus on Jutland. Here's your opportunity for another Danish sauna right in hotel.

Sonderborg, DK 6400

Baltic   Double with bath *$25*
Horuphav   Telephone (04)445200

For the truly adventurous driving on the tiny island of Als, off southern Jutland just north of German border. Right on water in attractive garden setting.

Spentrup, DK 8981

Hvidsten Kro   Double (no private baths) *$22*
Mariagervej 450   Telephone (06)477022

Historic inn dating from 1634, a landmark north of Jutland

town of Randers. A budget haven with but 12 rooms, no private baths.

Traneker, DK 8981

Traneker Gjaestgiveraard
Slotsgade 74

Double with bath *$37*
Telephone (09)591204

Another perfect destination for the wayfaring motorist, the island of Langeland off Fyn. Both island and inn a wonderland of flowers and shrubs.

Elizabeth / London

England

England still rates as everyone's favorite, at least with visitors from other English-speaking countries, and it's a shame so few of them (20% of Americans) venture beyond London. London Town is of course one of the earth's liveliest and most civilized cities, with every manner of diversion for its guests. Great restaurants serving foods from the world's four corners, marvelous theater at unbelievably low prices, museums, art, architecture, history on every street corner, music, in short, everything you could wish.

But the Lake District, Cotwolds, Cornwall-Devon, Wales, the south coast and just about any rural stretch of hedgerow-lined roadway in England offers you a look at the real "Tight Little Island," and missing it is your loss. Summer temperatures usually stay in the 60s, winters in the 40s, but wet going is a fact of life here. "Occasional bright intervals" as they say on the telly, which means you'll need a light rain-coat in between.

British Airways, Caledonian, Pan Am, TWA, American and *Delta* will get you there from the US. *BA, Air Canada* and *CP Air* from Canada. *BA* and *British Caledonian* are domestic airlines. *Godfrey Davis, Swan, Hertz, Avis* and *National* are the major car hire firms and a Ford *Fiesta* or *Escort* will cost you about $225, plus 15% tax, for a week of unlimited mileage. Fuel is currently $3.20 an Imperial gallon, 20% more than a US gallon.

Britain does not honor *Eurailpass* but has its own *BritRail* pass good for 7, 14, 21 or 30 days. It must be bought before you arrive in Britain and first-class costs for these periods are: $147, 219, 272, 317. Second-class fares are $162, 205 and 243 for the same periods and there are also senior citizen and youth prices. More information from *BritRail Travel* offices in major cities or your nearest *British Tourist Authority* office. Bus travel is a real bargain, being about half the cost of second-class rail, and there are *Coachmaster* tickets available for the same periods as *BritRail*.

British currency is the pound sterling, divided into 100 pence. Current value of the pound is $1.68, which makes the US dollar worth 60 pence. Banks are usually open from 9:30-3:30 Monday-Friday, shops from 9:00-5:30 six days. Voltages are from 200 to 250, 50 cycles, a real problem for 110-volt shavers and hair dryers as it is in most of Europe.

Good dining beyond London takes a bit of doing, with most smaller towns and villages having paltry few fine restaurants and some none at all. Hotel dining rooms and pubs are your best bet in the hustings and occasionally you will chance upon a truly outstanding inn that does wonders with seafood or game.

The food itself will delight the carnivore as "joints" of all manner and size are brought to table, plus steak-and-kidney pie, veal-and-ham pie, meat-stuffed Cornish pasties and usually delicious game pie. Seafood, particularly Dover sole and excellent oysters, graces a menu from time to time and the lowly fish-and-chips can be quite good, albeit a bit greasy.

Britons really know French wines and better restaurants usually have an impressive list, perfect company to the country's fine cheeses: the noble Stilton, Gloucester, Double Gloucester, Cheshire, Cheddar, Wensleydale, Caerphilly of Wales and the rare Blue Vinny of Dorset.

Even with the pound sterling sliding recently against the dollar, prices in Britain have climbed steadily and now must honestly be called expensive to the visitor. Countryside B&Bs still offer some measure of respite to those with tight budgets, small comfort indeed.

Hotels & Inns

Abbots Salford, Warwickshire

Salford Hall
Double with bath *$43-47*
Telephone (0386)870561

A stately manor house dating from 15th century in a garden setting. Only 10 rooms, six with private baths. All meals including teas.

Alfriston, East Sussex

Star Inn
Double with bath *$60-65*
High Street
Telephone (0323)870495

One of the loveliest small villages in south and the inn, dating from 1500, was once the stronghold of brigands bringing contraband from France, ironically built as a haven for pilgrims.

Bassenthwaite, Cumbria (Lake District)

Pheasant Inn

Double with bath *$52-54*
Telephone (059681)234

A 400-year-old coaching stop at north end of Bassenthwaite Lake. Patina of a fine old painting and bar to warm any traveler's heart.

Bath, Avon

Royal York
George Street

Double with bath *$50-62*
Telephone (0225)61541

A mid-18th-century bastion that came into its own during Victorian era. Sixty regal rooms and all amenities at town center.

Betws-y-Coed, Wales

Craig-y-Dderwen

Double with bath *$37*
Telephone (06902)293

Another stately Victorian country house in one of the most popular, and crowded, Welsh villages. Kitchen serves Conwy Valley game.

Royal Oak

Double with bath *$31-41*
Telephone (06902)219

Once a coaching stop, this one is larger than above with 33 rooms. Conwy Valley, Snowdonia make northern Wales a green wonderland.

Bodinnick, Cornwall

Old Ferry Inn

Double with bath *$55-60*
Telephone (072687)237

In all of Britain we've yet to find a more delightful place than this 400-year-old inn across river from Fowey. The 13th-century ferry (modernized only slightly) stops at your door, dining is heavenly, bar cozy and we can't wait for another return.

Bournemouth, Dorset

Chesterwood
East Overcliff

Double with bath *$41-48*
Telephone (0202) 28057

Bournemouth about as far as day-trippers from London get and they come in droves. Pool and marvelous views here, dancing.

Bourton-on-the-Water, Gloucestershire (Cotswolds)

Riverside

Double (no private baths) *$33*
Telephone (0451)20892

Modest guest house B&B fronting the tiny stream that flows through village. Bourton usually crowded so here are a few alternatives.

Old Manse

Double with bath *$66-70*
Telephone (0451)20082

This 200-year-old house on banks of Windrush has one of Cotswolds' better dining rooms. We remember well a delectable roast grouse.

Old New Inn
High Street

Double with bath *$46*
Telephone (0451)20467

Like many of the town's houses, this one is made of warm, golden Cotswold stone. Private baths a scarcity here, so call.

Braithwaite, Cumbria (Lake District)

Ivy House

Double with bath *$65-74*
Telephone (059682)338

Price a bit steep, but we can attest to the value at this 1630 country house that glistens with fine furnishings, china, silver and care. They'll prepare a picnic for your Lakeland hike.

Branscombe, Devon

Mason Arms

Double with bath *$51-57*
Telephone (029780)300

South Devon one of England's most bucolic regions and Branscombe an idyllic village. Inn a 14th-century smugglers' meeting place, now noted for fine food, particularly its Sunday lunches.

Broughton-in-Furness, Cumbria (Lake District)

Eccles Riggs

Double with bath *$41-46*
Telephone (06576)398

Broughton on south coast of Lake District at head of beautiful bay. Only eight rooms at this Victorian mansion, commendable food.

Burford, Oxfordshire (Cotswolds)

Bay Tree
Sheep Street

Double with bath *$46-60*
Telephone (099382)3137

It's difficult to forget our stop at this 16th-century mansion with its marvelous old furnishings, cozy fireplaces, bar giving onto a deep garden, and memorable food served by candlelight.

Lamb Inn
Sheep Street

Double with bath *$48-55*
Telephone (099382)3155

Many claim Burford to be Britain's loveliest medieval wool town. Certainly it has another wondrous inn in the 15th-century Lamb.

Caernarfon, Wales

Stables Hotel
South of town 3 miles

Double with bath *$54-62*
Telephone (0286)6043

This 19th-century stable block was turned into a distinctive hotel/restaurant a decade ago and now draws raves from guests. Caernarfon Castle makes visit to the town almost a must.

Cambridge, Cambridgeshire

Belle Vue Guest House   Double (no private baths) *$37*
33 Chesterton Road   Telephone (0223)51859

A sparkling B&B across from lovely park with perfect location for walking the colleges of this ancient, tranquil university town.

Arundel House   Double with bath *$48-58*
53 Chesterton Road   Telephone (0223)67701

Another old Victorian a few steps away and also just across from Jesus Green. Bright, cheerful and all meals may be taken here.

Canterbury, Kent (see also Fordwich)

Falstaff   Double with bath *$52-55*
St. Dunstan's Street   Telephone (0227)62138

An old coaching stop since 1403, this small place still retains a goodly measure of its heritage. Sturdy English meals, worthy of its namesake, served in a room where Chaucer's pilgrims ate.

Abby Gate   Double (no private baths) *$37*
7 North Lane   Telephone (0227)68770

Those same pilgrims may have had the problem we did in walking the crooked hallways of this fine old place near *Falstaff*.

Carmarthen, Wales

Boar's Head Inn   Double with bath *$40*
Lammas Street   Telephone (0267)6043

South Wales is hardly the slag heap some proclaim and this old market town, set in Dylan Thomas country, is worthy of a visit. Sunday lunch in *Boar Head's* provincial dining room a delight.

Cartmel, Cumbria (Lake District)

Priory   Double with bath *$38-44*
The Square   Telephone (044854)267

This vine-covered early Georgian house is named after the village's 12th-century priory church. Lunch, dinner, teas a convenience and quite good.

Chester, Cheshire

Ye Olde King's Head   Double (no private baths) *$44-48*
48 Lower Bridge Street   Telephone (0244)24855

Built as a private home in 1520. A magnificent little place with black and white timbered facade in Tudor style of Chester's famous Rows. Rates include full English breakfast.

Chipping Camden, Gloucestershire (Cotswolds)

Noel Arms   Double with bath *$55-63*
High Street   Telephone (0386)840317

A 14th-century coaching stop that retains every bit of the character of this medieval wool town (chipping means market). You won't forget a stay, or meals in timbered dining room.

Seymour House   Double with bath *$40-46*
High Street   Telephone (0386)840429

Another charming place that has long been a favorite of ours. Terrace dining under an arbor, quiet beyond belief, no children.

Coventry, West Midlands

Beechwood   Double with bath *$40-43*
Sandpits Lane, Keresley   Telephone (020333)4243
3 miles NW of Coventry

Coventry's new cathedral, one of the most glorious structures in all Christendom, is reason enough for a visit, but you'll be happier outside town. Dining room menu offers relief from English fare with Continental dishes.

Dover, Kent

Granham Webb   Double with bath *$38-50*
161 Folkestone Road   Telephone (0304)201897

An old Victorian carriage house that draws locals for its food. One reader wrote a two-page letter on the carbonnade of beef.

Ettington, Warwickshire

Chase County House   Double with bath *$48*
Banbury Road   Telephone (0789)740000

Stratford residents complain that their town is overcrowded. True. So repair to this 14-acre estate in a hamlet on the Stour River south of town. Few rooms but fine food in old country house.

Fishguard, Wales

Cartref Inn   Double (no private baths) **$33-36**
High Street   Telephone (0348)872430

Fishguard the coastal departure point for Ireland's Rosslare ferry. This small one at town center serves authentic Welsh food.

Fordwich, Kent

George and Dragon   Double with bath *$47-51*
3 miles outside Canterbury   Telephone (0227)710661

A magnificent, rambling 16th-century coaching stop on the Stour River (Caesar's galleys landed here) that has never failed to enchant us. Glorious food and a wine list the equal of any.

Fowey, Cornwall

Riverside Inn   Double with bath *$46-63*
Passage Street   Telephone (072683)2275

This cozy little place leans out over the River Fowey (Foy) just across from Bodinnick's *Old Ferry Inn*. Excellent dining room and away from crowds that jam town during summer season.

Grassmere, Cumbria (Lake District)

Chestnut Villa   Double (no private baths) *$36*
On A-591   Telephone (09665)218

Neat and sparkling B&B just a step down road from *Swan*, where you may take other meals after *Chestnut's* English breakfast.

Swan   Double with bath *$56-65*
On A-591   Telephone (09665)551

Wordsworth, who lived nearby in Dove Cottage, wrote: "Who does not know the famous Swan?" You will be equally impressed by this warm and friendly place and its fine collection of pewter, copperware, china and shining horse brasses. Great pub too.

Henley-on-Thames, Oxfordshire

Tudor Rooms   Double (no private baths) *$38*
40 Hart Street   Telephone (04912)4261

A few attractive B&B rooms in this medieval building that also houses a tea shop downstairs. Short walk to serene Thameside.

Red Lion   Double with bath *$50-58*
Hart Street   Telephone (04912)2161

Henley's choice hotel, a fine old building overlooking the Thames. Town jammed during Royal Regatta rowing event first week in July.

Horton-cum-Studley, Oxfordshire

Studley Priory   Double with bath *$48-78*
6 miles NE of Oxford   Telephone (086735)203

A Tudor/Elizabethan manor set in a huge estate with lovely gardens. Room prices in the main house with antique furnishings are the more expensive, those in the stable building less so.

Lanreath, Cornwall

Punch Bowl Inn

Double with bath *$48-58*
Telephone (0503)20218

This inn has been welcoming visitors since 1615 or there-abouts and is known for its homey atmosphere and authentic Cornish food. It's tarted up a bit and the souvenir counter hardly an addition.

Llanrwst, Wales (Conwy Valley)

Pen Loyn Farm
Just outside town

Double (no private baths) *$35*
Telephone (0492)640631

A family owned working farm with everyone pitching in. Rolling countryside wondrous and chatter of Welsh a musical delight.

Eagles Inn
Town center

Double with bath *$40-42*
Telephone (0482)640454

A comfortable old Welsh hotel on banks of Conwy River near market square in this fetching little town. Praiseworthy high teas.

London

Elizabeth
38 Eccleston Square
London SW1V 1PB

Double with bath *$54-62*
Telephone (01)8286812

A small but stately Georgian townhouse overlooking an attractive garden square and walking distance to Victoria Station, airline terminal and Belgravia. Friendliest proprietor and our own favorite.

Averard
10 Lancaster Gate
London W2 3LH

Double with bath *$47*
Telephone (01)7238877

Another old converted townhouse across from Kensington Gardens and steps from lively 17th-century *Swan Pub*. Modest, as is price.

Westland
154 Bayswater Road
London W2 4HP

Double with bath *$48-58*
Telephone (01) 2299191

Our decades of staying at the *Westland* have always been pleasant. Also just across from Kensington Gardens, near underground station.

Willet
32 Sloan Gardens
London SW1 W8DJ

Double with bath *$43-49*
Telephone (01)7300634

A small, modest and difficult to find place south of Hyde Park just off Sloan Square. Good location, value at London prices.

Number Sixteen
16 Sumner Place
London SW7 3EG

Double with bath *$56-82*
Telephone (01)5895232

The absolute ultimate in B&Bs, a small charmer that you may very well choose to regard as your home away from home in London Town.

Lynton, Devon

Lynton Cottage
North Walk

Double with bath *$45-50*
Telephone (05985)2342

Very much the English holiday hotel, high on a cliff with awesome view of Bristol Channel, commendable dining, great walking country.

Mousehole, Cornwall

Lobster Pot

Double with bath *$35-70*
Telephone (073673)251

A delightful 15th-century inn that was once a fisherman's cottage on a harbor at the tip of Cornwall's Lands End. Star in its crown is the rustic dining room with heavenly local seafood.

Oxford, Oxfordshire (see also Horton-cum-Studley)

The Galaxie Double (no private baths) *$38*
180 Banbury Road Telephone (0865)55688

Prepare for a welcome as friendly as you'll ever see and total immersion into British B&B scene, with huge English breakfast, spotless rooms and baths, and "telly" with other guests for evening news.

Old Parsonage Double with bath *$42-48*
1 Banbury Road Telephone (0865)54843

Fine old historic hostelry that was once, alas, one of our budget havens. Terribly popular now, so by all means book soon.

Penzance, Cornwall

Union Inn Double with bath *$46-50*
Chapel Street Telephone (0736)2319

Another one at the tip of Cornwall, this a modernized old coaching stop at town center within walking distance of active harbor.

Portsmouth, Hampshire

Keppels Head Double with bath *$65*
The Hard Telephone (0705)21954

You'll be overcome with *Rule Britannia* at this very Royal Navy place right on the port. Nelson's flagship a half-block away, superior dining and a bar so nautical it'll make you seasick.

Salsbury, Wilshire

King's Arms Double with bath *$46*
St. John's Street Telephone (0722)27629

Tudor inn all timbered beams, wattle and daub, with excellent food and the coziest of pubs. Salsbury's oldest as the crooked stairs and "priest's hiding hole" in dining room attest. Visit Stonehenge and town's magnificent cathedral from this charming old place.

Shaftsbury, Dorset

Grosvenor · Double with bath *$54-64*
The Commons · Telephone (0747)2282

An old coaching stop brought up-to-date with fine dining room serving one of best cream teas in Dorset. We always stop here.

Stratford-upon-Avon, Warwickshire (see also Ettington)

White Swan · Double with bath *$52-64*
Rother Street · Telephone (0789)297022

A warm and friendly 15th-century inn with murals in the beamed lounge dating back to its opening. You might expect to find Shakespeare stalking the halls here. Breakfasts are superb.

Grosvenor House · Double with bath *$45-57*
Warwick Road · Telephone (0798)69213

An old favorite for its location within walking of Royal Shakespeare Theater on river. Cheerful but occasionally tour-jammed.

Stow-on-the-Wold, Gloucestershire (Cotswolds)

King's Arms · Double with bath *$36-44*
Market Square · Telephone (0451)30364

Two of our Stow visits have ended at the *King's Arms*, a quaint Tudor inn and one of several good ones right on Market Square.

Swansea, Wales (The Mumbles)

Mermaid · Double with bath *$46-52*
688 Mumbles Road, · Telephone (0792)68125
Southend, Mumbles

An architectural melange fronting a most comfortable and homey place on "beach" of Swansea Bay. Friendliest of owners and a warm, pleasant bar where Dylan Thomas surely spent his visits.

Wells, Somerset

Swan   Double with bath *$70*
9 Sadler Street   Telephone (0749)78877

One of our favorite small hotels in all Europe, a 16th-century coaching stop right on medieval Market Square beside the exquisite 13th-century cathedral. Crackling fireplaces, four-poster bed upstairs, tremendous food, service quiet but crisp. Inquire about their Christmas-week program, all this plus holly and stuffed goose!

Star   Double with bath *$55*
High Street   Telephone (0749)73055

Another coaching inn built in the same century, this one a bit more modest but still a warren of timber beams and rustic rooms.

Windemere, Cumbria (Lake District)

Cranleigh   Double with bath *$48-54*
Kendal Road,   Telephone (09662)3293
Bowness-on-Windemere

Few rooms here but value is excellent in the popular (and now crowded year-round) Lake District. Near bay and has weekly rates.

Polar Ounasvaara / Rovaniemi

Finland

Finland, *Suomi* to its natives, is the least visited of Scandinavian countries and that is a pity. For here is a sparkling country of virgin forests, tumbling rivers, crystal clear air, lovely low mountains and almost 60,000 shimmering lakes just waiting for the adventurous traveler. It's a young country, independent only since 1917 after centuries of Swedish and Russian rule. Its youth is probably best expressed by truly remarkable contemporary architecture and city planning, a European leader in both. About 4.7 million Finns, almost all of whom have blond hair and ice-blue eyes, are spread thin throughout the country, only 35 per square mile. They are sturdy, vigorous and healthy beyond belief, yet manage to consume more alcohol per capita than any other Europeans. Their language is an absolute mind-bender but, as in most of Scandinavia, English will get you by much of the time.

Central Finland seems to have more lakes than dry ground and the word *suomi* actually means swamp. But the lakes are magnificent to behold and several good north-south highways split the area, with secondary roads forming a cobweb to every lakeshore. Finnish Lapland above the Arctic Circle is a stunning but remote region. Only two roads of any size run north-south, and east-west travel is difficult. Rail service stops at Rovaniemi on the Circle, with daily flights from Helsinki to Ivalo 185 miles farther north on the Russian border. From here on it's car, bus or dogsled.

SAS and *Finnair* will fly you there from the US and from Canada. *Finnair's* domestic system has a very popular *Holiday Ticket*, good for unlimited travel for 15 days and the cost is only $200. *Avis, Hertz, FinnRent, Europcar* and *InterRent* will provide a *Ford Fiesta, Fiat 127* or *VW Polo* for about $320 per week unlimited mileage, plus 16% tax. Plan on paying about $2.30 per gallon for super fuel.

Finland honors *Eurailpass* and has its own *Finnrail Pass* for 8, 15, and 22 days of unlimited travel. Cost in 1983 of first-class for these periods: $90, 132, and 177; second-class: $60, 88 and 118. Finland also participates in the *Nordturist Med Tag* Scandinavian railway plan with Sweden, Norway and Denmark with 21 days of first or second-class travel for $227 or $151, children half that. A full month will cost you $285 first-class, $189 second, and tickets are available in most European railway stations. Bus travel is the only access to many Finnish towns and Finland's buses are as modern and fast as any in Europe.

Currency unit is the *markka*, divided into 100 *penni*, and it's now worth about 18 cents US or 5.50 to the dollar. Banks are open from 9:15-4:15, five days, store hours 8:30-5:00 weekdays, only until 2:00 p.m. Saturdays. Voltage is 220, 60 cycle. Summer temperatures are in the high 50s and 60s, November through March in the 30s and lower.

Vital, vigorous, virile are the words for Finnish cooking, just as they are for that other Finnish tradition, the *sauna*. Pork and mutton sausages, gigantic smoked herring, cured leg of lamb, reindeer steaks, strong cheeses, coarse bread, delectable crayfish, fish and potato soup, and all of it washed down with torrents of beer, mead, vodka and white wine.

Finns have their own version of *smorgasbord* and it's likely that you will meet several of the above dishes on one table. Mushrooms and berries play large roles in Finland's cuisine and they are plentiful indeed. One of the sturdiest and most popular dishes is the *kalakukko*, a provincial offering from central Finland that can weigh ten pounds. Chunks of pork and whole, small fish are imbedded in a gigantic ball of rye dough and baked. *Patakukko* is a casserole version of the same dish, the one you are likely to meet in restaurants.

Finland is still a moderately priced country to visit, certainly by northern Europe-Scandinavian standards, and the northern provinces can be very gentle on your budget.

Hotels & Inns

Hameenlinna

Kaupunginhotelli   Double with bath *$40-54*
Rauhankatu 3   Telephone (9)1723561
13100 Hameenlinna 10

Small, good central location and favorite meeting place of locals in gateway city to Finland's lovely lakeland north of Helsinki.

Rantasipi Aulanko   Double with bath *$68*
13230 Aulanko   Telephone (9)1729521

Right on shore of lake in parklike setting just outside Hameenlinna. Not plush, just a country holiday hotel with superior food and enough recreation facilities to keep you exhausted for weeks.

Helsinki

Marttahotelli
Uudenmaankatu 24
Nylandsgatan
00120 Helsinki 12

Double with bath *$42-49*
Telephone (9)0646211

A recent visit confirmed that our favorite small Helsinki hotel is still least expensive. Excellent staff, fine breakfasts.

Helka
P. Rautatickatu 23
North Jarnvagsgaten
00100 Helsinki 10

Double with bath *$52-72*
Telephone (9)0440581

A cheerful, Finnish modern hotel with good central location near airline terminal, train and bus stations. Pleasant dining room.

Hospiz
Vuorikatu 17
Berggaton
00100 Helsinki 10

Double with bath *$50-65*
Telephone (9)0170481

Another neat and crisp place with equally good location. Rooms are small and simple, dining room will serve you fast and well.

Kalastajatorppa
Kalastajatopantie 1
Fiskartorpsvagen
00330 Helsinki 33

Double with bath *$85*
Telephone (9)0488011

One can hardly believe the name "Fisherman's Cottage" for this very contemporary luxury hotel on a lakelike bay of the Baltic just outside city. Separate circular restaurant one of Finland's finest, serving us best food and wine of a recent trip.

Jyvaskyla

Rentukka
Taitoniekantu 9
40740 Juvaskyla 74

Double with bath *$30*
Telephone (9)41252211

Hard to believe this price for room with kitchenette, even if it is a student dorm a mile from south Finland university town. Many Scandinavians use these "summer hotels" for vacationing.

Naantali

Kultainen Aurinko Double with bath *$37*
Kalevanniemi Telephone (9)21752961
21100 Naantali

The president of Finland has his summer home in this charming little harbor town near Turku. Hotel not far from beach with pool, sauna. Excellent food in *Restaurant Kalatrappi* nearby.

Rovaniemi (Lapland)

Domus Arctica Double with bath *$25*
Ratakatu 8 Telephone (9)912981
96100 Rovaniemi 10

Another soothing room bill at this summer hotel a half-mile from town center. All these places are bright and cheerful. Most have full restaurants, this one serving Lapp specialties.

Ounasvaara Double with bath *$48-55*
96400 Rovaniemi 40 Telephone (9)913771

Usual clean Finnish architecture and glassed-in dining room has stunning view of Lapland lakes and forests. Try the reindeer steaks, salmon and cloudberries, the Finnish national fruit.

Sodankyla-Luosto (Lapland)

Luostonhovi Double with bath *$42*
99600 Sodankyla-Luosto Telephone (9)9344200

Eighty miles due north of Rovaniemi and the Arctic Circle motorists will find this rustic log lodge set in a forest wonderland. Glorious food smothered in wild mushrooms, and *Reindeer Tears* (Cointreau and Finnish vodka). They were so good I can hardly read my notes.

Tampere

Victoria   Double with bath *$42*
Itsenaisyydenkatu 1   Telephone (9)3130640
33100 Tampere 10

Rather boxy, as Finnish hotels can be, but ultra-modern and most convenient to railway station and bus terminal. Choice of saunas!

Domus   Double with bath *$31*
Pellervonkatu 9   Telephone (9)3150000
33540 Tampere 54

Another student dormitory used as summer hotel, this one huge and with its own sauna and pool. Convenient location.

Turku (see also Naantali)

Hamburger Bors   Double with bath *$57-64*
Kauppiaskatu 6   Telephone (9)21511211
Kopmamsgatan
20101 Turku 10

A quarter-century favorite of ours in center near colorful market square. Dining room deserves praise for its treatment of grouse, pheasant and heavenly lingonberries with whipped cream.

Domus Aboensis   Double with bath *$35*
Piispankatu 10   Telephone (9)2129470
20500 Turku 50

Like all summer hotels, this one open only from June 1 to August 31. Near Old Town, the Sibelius Museum and Aurajoki River through town.

Petit Coq aux Champs / Campigny

France

Tunneled vision affects visitors to France as well as England: many cannot see beyond the City of Light. Yet much — indeed most — of France is beautiful enough to draw millions of Europeans on holiday each year, not to mention an even greater number of Frenchmen who consider their country the Continent's most inviting vacation spot and set out to prove it on the roads of France every July and August. Satiate yourself on Parisian delights, then find more of the same in Burgundy, the Loire, Rhone and Dordogne valleys, Provence, Alsace and its lovely Vosges mountains or in the Basque region of the southwest. Art, architecture and that infectious French *joie de vivre* are spread in equal measure throughout the country, while superlative food and wine await you in the meanest French village. One of France's best restaurants, by acclamation, is located in

Vienne, an otherwise undistinguished town just south of Lyon.

Air France flys from the United States and Canada, along with *TWA, Pan Am* and *Air Canada* from their respective countries. Once there, *Avis, Europcar* and *Hertz* will have a *Ford Fiesta, Renault 5* or small *Peugeot* 4-door waiting for you costing about $185 per week unlimited mileage, plus 17.6% tax. Super fuel is currently 4.69 francs per liter or $2.46 per gallon. *Air Inter* along with *Air France* are domestic airlines serving mainland cities and Corsica.

SNCF is the French National Railways system, with offices in New York, Chicago, San Francisco, Beverly Hills, Montreal and Toronto. They honor *Eurailpass* and have their own *France Vacances* pass, as near a total transportation package as you will find in Europe. It's available for 7, 15 or 30 days, first and second-class, and 1983 prices are $170, 220 and 345 or $115, 150 and 230 for the periods. But you also get a free pass from either of Paris' two airports into town, a free Metro and bus ticket in Paris for 4 or 7 days, depending upon whether you bought a ticket for 7 days or 15-30. Plus a 10% discount on *SNFC's* bus excursions and also a free rental car for 1 or 2 days, again depending on whether your *first-class* ticket is for 7-15 or 30 days. Purchase *France Vacances* pass through offices listed in our last pages.

The *franc* is France's currency, divided into 100 *centimes*, and now worth approximately 18 cents or 5.50 per US dollar. Banking hours are 9:00-4:00 but opening on Monday and closing on Saturday are at noon. Store hours are 9:00-6:30 with noon opening Monday and many open Saturday evenings. Voltage in France is 220.

France has the best food in the world, bar none, and if there is one thing a Frenchman will not abide it's mediocrity at the table. They also *enjoy* dining, sampling from each other's plates, carrying on animated conversation as the Italians do and generally treating mealtime as a festive and happy occasion. All of this works to your advantage as it is very, very difficult to have a really bad meal in France.

More than 400 varieties of cheeses and an infinitely greater number of "local" wines are waiting for you on the tables of France. We have tried our share of both with remarkably few disappointments. Regional and provincial specialties are far too numerous to mention here, but the oysters and seafood of Brittany, Normandy's lamb and cream sauces, the sausages, sauerkraut and fine beer of Alsace, Burgundy's beef and crayfish, Languedoc's hearty *cassoulets* and the equally robust *bouillabaisse* of Provence, all make new converts to French provincial cuisine.

The *mystique*, flavor and all-round joy of a visit to France can be elusive to some, but we consider it one of the most beautiful and satisfying countries in Europe. While prices continue to rise, thanks to the government's removal of many price controls in late 1982, France is still a remarkable value and we consider food and lodging outside Paris and other big cities as low-to-medium-priced. So forget *l'addition* and rejoice that you are there enjoying the earth's most glorious food.

Hotels & Inns

Aix-en-Provence, 13100 Provence

Le Prieure	Double with bath *$30*
Route des Alpes	Telephone (42)210523
Mile north of town	

A bright and cheerful little place with formal gardens, lots of flowers and decorated as only the French can, with matching slip covers, valence, bedspreads and perhaps wallpaper. Breakfasts only here.

Angers, 4900 Loire

Saint-Jacques	Double with bath *$28*
83 rue Saint-Jacques	Telephone (41)485105

Admirable small hotel with 19 rooms, fine dining, as such

hotels in France often have. Pleasant and altogether comfortable place to use as base for your visits to Loire chateaux.

Arles, 13200 Provence

Mireille   Double with bath *$36-40*
2 Place St-Pierre   Telephone (90)937074

Across the Rhone from the town's beautiful Roman theater and arena, this one has a cooling pool for when the Mediterranean sun boils down. Lovely setting, excellent restaurant.

Avallon, 89200 Burgundy

Manoir du Morvan   Double with bath *$28*
7 Route de Paris   Telephone (86)340030

Quiet and on the outskirts of town. No restaurant here but you will find superb dining at the *Poste* or *Restaurant Morvan.*

Hostellerie de la Poste   *Double with bath $48-65*
13 Place Vauban   Telephone (86)340612

C'est formidable. Not only is it one of France's most charming inns, the restaurant rates raves from everyone. Worth every *centime.*

Avignon, 84000 Provence

Auberge de France   Double with bath *$28*
28 Place Horloge   Telephone (90)825886

Marvelous location in center of old walled city, but you might request a quiet rear room. Reputation rests with great food.

La Baule, 44500 Brittany

Palmeraie   Double with bath *$30-32*
7 Allee Cormorans   Telephone (40)602441

Just two blocks from Atlantic in resort near St. Nazaire, this most attractive place has 23 rooms, each with bath, and a feeling of bright cheerfulness throughout.

Beaune, 44500 Burgundy

Auberge Bourguignonne   Double with bath *$29*
4 Place Madeleine   Telephone (80)222353

All our visits to this warm little place on an old market square
just outside the town's medieval walls have been memorable
for the best of Burgundy's food, wines and friendly service.

De la Poste   Double with bath *$65-85*
5 Boulevard Clemenceau   Telephone (80)220811

Everything you could hope for in a lodging for the night,
elegance, total comfort, plus the best table in town. Try the
crayfish!

Biarritz, 64200 Aquitaine (Pyrenees)

Mirador   Double with bath *$35*
10 Place Sainte-Eugenie   Telephone (59)241381

Convenient to port and casinos, for those with spare *francs,*
and its *Rotisserie Coq Hardi* will overwhelm you with fine
Basque food.

Biriatou, 64700 Aquitaine (Pyrenees)

Bakea   Double with bath *$30*
Road between Hendaye   Telephone (59)207636
and St-Jean-de-Luz

Beautiful setting in the Basque corner of SW France with a
chef noted for his preparation of this unique Spanish/French
cuisine.

Blois, 41000 Loire

De la Loire   Double with bath *$28*
8 rue de-Lattre-de-Tassigny   Telephone (54)742660

A no-nonsense little hotel on a street running along the
Loire, its reputation for solid comfort augmented by a
masterful chef.

Bordeaux, 33000 Aquitaine

La Reserve   Double with bath *$35-55*
74 Avenue du Bourgailh   Telephone (56)451328
33600 Pessac

Set in a heavenly parklike reserve on lake in suburb of l'Alouette. Elegant dining, accompanied by Bordeaux's best.

Bourg-en-Bresse, 01000 Rhone-Loire

Hotel de France   Double with bath *$35-38*
19 Place Bernard   Telephone (74)233024

An older place in center of town. Dining room prepares famous *poulet de Bresse* admirably, but for the best try for reservations at *Auberge Bressane* at 116 Boulevard Brou.

Campigny, 27500 Normandy

Petit Coq aux Champs   Double with bath *$40-58*
4 miles S of Pont-Audemer   Telephone (32)410419

This delightful little 19th-century cottage has just about everything going for it: tranquil grounds awash in flowers; excellent Normandy food; 11 pleasant rooms and a heated swimming pool. Breakfast is included.

Cannes, Riviera — 06400 Cote d'Azur

Touring   Double with bath *$35*
9 rue Hoche   Telephone (93)383440

Excellent location near *La Croisette* seaside promenade, railway station and casino. Prices tend to rise during July-August.

P.L.M.   Double with bath *$32*
3 rue Hoche   Telephone (93)383119

Same good location as above, both with 30 rooms and serve only breakfasts. But the prices are certainly right for Cannes.

La Madone   Double with bath *$38-55*
5 Avenue Justina   Telephone (93)435787

A very peaceful place with 20 rooms, all having baths, east

of town center. No meals, but clutch of restaurants along port.

Carcassonne, 11000 Languedoc-Roussillon

| Donjon | Double with bath *$38* |
| 22 rue Ducumte Roger | Telephone (68)251113 |

Very typical and the only hotel within medieval walls of the Old City. Readers never fail to praise friendly staff.

| Le Montmorency | Double with bath *$28* |
| 2 rue Camille-St-Saens | Telephone (68)251992 |

Very modest and small (12 rooms) with no restaurant. Try the rustic but excellent *Languedoc* for duck and other game.

Chagny, 71150 Burgundy

Les Capucines	Double with bath *$28*
Route de Chalon	Telephone (85)870817
9 miles S of Beaune	

A charming old farmhouse with courtyard right out of another time. Simple rooms but what food! We remember well a house pate wrapped in *brioche* and beautifully prepared Burgundian *escargots*.

Cluny, 71250 Burgundy

| Modern | Double with bath *$30* |
| Pont de l'Etang | Telephone (85)590565 |

Dining room alone worth half-mile drive from this delightful village. Site on river marvelous, but the food draws us back.

Deauville, , 14800 Normandy

| Le Nid d'Ete | Double with bath *$32* |
| 121 Avenue de la Republique | Telephone (3)883667 |

This turn-of-century resort still has an elegant air about it. Hotel has good location and restaurant usual fixed-price menu.

Gevrey-Chambertin, 21220 Burgundy

Les Grands Crus   Double with bath *$32*
Route des Grands Crus   Telephone (80)343415

Dead center of some of the world's best vineyards, most rooms with window boxes overflowing with flowers. A perfect gem.

Honfleur, 14600 Normandy

Grand Cour   Double (no private baths) *$34*
Equemauville-Cote de Grace   Telephone (31)890469

You won't worry about the lack of private baths in this fine old estate looking down on Honfleur. Half-pension rates attractive.

Juan les Pins, 06160 Riviera — Cote d'Azur

Pre Catelan   Double with bath *$38*
22 Avenue des Lauriers   Telephone (93)610511

A neat villa that is less than 200 yards from beach and casino. You'll enjoy meals on terrace, surrounded by flowers and shrubs.

Les Eyzies, 24620 Aquitaine (Dordogne)

Cro-Magnon   Double with bath *$45-52*
                     Telephone (53)069706

A delightful old house covered with vines in one of France's most scenic regions. Flowers everywhere and very best kitchen.

Lyon, 69002 Rhone — Loire

PLM Terminus   Double with bath *$40-52*
12 cours Verdun   Telephone (7)8375811
Perrache Station

Large but homey 19th-century hotel practically in railway station. France's beautiful, 165 mph *TGV* trains will whisk you down from Paris in 2½ hours. Dining room can hold its head high in this city noted for three-star restaurants and talented Paul Bocuse.

Macon, 71000 Burgundy

La Savoie   Double with bath *$32*
87 rue Rambuteau   Telephone (85)384222

Good central location not far from station, rooms comfortable enough and restaurant always has attractive fixed-price menu.

Marseille, 13000 Provence

Residence du Vieux Port   Double with bath *$35-45*
18 quai Port   Telephone (91)907911

A comfortable older place with room balconies overlooking the Old Port where you'll find any number of great seafood *bistros.*

Megeve, 74120 Alpes-du-Nord

Au Vieux Moulin   Double with bath *$48-52*
Avenue Ambroise-Martin   Telephone (50)212229

At village center with an air of grace, good meals and even a heated pool for the nippy altitude.

Chalet des Fleurs   Double with bath *$18-22*
Route de Sallanches   Telephone (50)212146
Half-mile NE of village

Our readers have been happy for years at this *Logis de France.* Full or half-pension good idea if you're here awhile.

Mont Saint-Michel, 50116 Normandy

Mouton Blanc   Double with bath *$26*
                                   Telephone (33)601408

Modest but comfortable place with most obliging owners. They might even whip you up an omelet if you can't find one on the Mont.

Nice, 06000 Riviera — Cote d'Azur
(see also Villefranche-sur-Mer)

| Oasis | Double with bath *$28-32* |
| 23 rue Gounod | Telephone (93)881229 |

Our readers on limited budgets have found the hotel name
very descriptive for many years. Close to railway station.

| Durante | Double with bath *$28-32* |
| 16 rue Durante | Telephone (93)888440 |

Durante and *Oasis* share more than a common price scale.
Both are modest and near station, but no meals at this one.

Nimes, 30000 Languedoc

| Le Louvre | Double with bath *$32-34* |
| 2 sq. Couronne | Telephone (66)672275 |

Another no-nonsense place between a church and lovely
small square, just a step from the town's glorious Roman
arena.

Paris

d'Isley	Double with bath *$38*
29 rue Jacob	Telephone (1)3266441
Paris 75006	

A pair of sprightly laurel bushes frame the entryway and
again proclaim *d'Isley* the victor, as it has been for many
years, in our annual search for the perfect Parisian small
hotel. St-Germain-des-Pres neighborhood the greatest, a
beehive of fine *bistros,* street markets and Left Bank action.
Alors, we love it.

Angleterre	Double with bath *$44-48*
44 rue Jacob	Telephone (1)2603472
Paris 75006	

Former British embassy was long ago turned into fine hotel
with a steady following. Flowered central breakfast patio
delightful.

Scandinavia   Double with bath *$40*
27 rue de Tournon   Telephone (1)3296720
Paris 75006

A warm and intimate 17th-century inn, this one the coziest of small hotels with beamed ceilings everywhere, marvelous furnishings. Hard to book.

St. Simon   Double with bath *$65*
14 rue de St. Simon   Telephone (1)5483566
Paris 75007

Small but stately town house set back in a garden. All 34 rooms have baths here. No restaurant, nor do our other Paris hotels.

Solferino   Double with bath *$40*
91 rue de Lille   Telephone (1)7058554
Paris 75007

Another simple but comfortable place on a street paralleling the Seine. Cross the bridge and you're in the Louvre!

Lutece   Double with bath *$46*
65 rue Saint-Louis-en-l'Ile   Telephone (1)3257976
Paris 75004

Looking a bit like an Amsterdam canal house of the 17th century, this exquisite place is on the main but narrow street that runs down the middle of Ile Saint-Louis in the Seine behind Notre Dame. Twin sisters, the *Deux-Iles* and *Saint-Louis* nearby and owned by the same family, drop a notch in prices.

Perpignon, 66000 Languedoc-Roussillon

De la Poste   Double with bath *$20-24*
6 rue Fabriques-Nabot   Telephone (68)344253

Good central location near the cathedral in this town near the Spanish border. Dining room usually has a robust *cassoulet* on menu.

Plascassiere, 06870 Provence

La Tourmaline	Double with bath *$30-32*
Quartier Masseboeuf	Telephone (93)671008
Route D4	

About 14 miles into the hills above Cannes you'll find this small gem two miles east of Grasse. A country place with very few rooms, superior dining, just the place to relax for a few days.

Ribeauville, 68150 Alsace

Ville de Nancy	Double with bath *$24*
7 Grand Rue	Telephone (89)736057

A perfectly charming town in the midst of vineyards with Teutonic overtones of the region. You'll enjoy the *choucroute garnie* and other hearty Alsatian food served here. Good beer too.

Pepiniere	Double with bath *$38-40*
Route de St-Marie-aux-Mines	Telephone (89)736414
Three miles NW of town	

Take a beautiful drive up into the Vosges Forest to this quiet and peaceful hotel noted for its fine food of the region. Fall is perfect time for Ribeauville as they bring in area's grapes.

Rouen, 76000 Normandy

De la Cathedrale	Double with bath *$30-34*
12 rue St-Romain	Telephone (35)715795

This small and delightful place has been in our book for years and everyone loves it as much as we do. Just steps from the city's magnificent cathedral. No restaurant here but nearby *Dufour* will keep you happy.

Saint-Hippolyte, 68590 Alsace

Aux Ducs de Lorraine	Double with bath *$40-45*
16 Route du Vin	Telephone (89)730009

Again, right in the vineyards. This enormous and imposing

place is also noted for its restaurant serving the heartiest of Alsatian dishes. We remember well a venison lunch with our full quota of wondrous local wine.

St-Jean-de-Luz, 64500 Aquitaine

Du Jardin   Double (no private baths) *$20*
5 rue Loquin   Telephone (59)260551

Probably the most modest place we have for France, but it's in the middle of this gay holiday port on the Spanish border, with simple but delicious food served in outdoor patio.

St-Jean-Pied-de-Port, Aquitaine (Pyrenees)

Des Pyrenees   Double with bath *$25-32*
19 Place General-de-Gaulle   Telephone (59)370101

Another colorful holiday town, this one in the Pyrenees just across Spanish border from Pamplona. Hotel, on main square beside river, has town's finest restaurant. Buy your rope-sole shoes in St-Jean!

Strasbourg, 67000 Alsace

Gutenberg   Double with bath *$28*
31 rue des Serruriers   Telephone (88)321715

An 18th-century hotel that still evokes the aura of that time of elegance. Best location in this fascinating city, just a block from its marvelous cathedral. If you've been saving your *francs,* dine at *Le Crocodile* and then stuff your luggage with Strasbourg's *pate-de-fois-gras* as we did.

Villefranche-sur-Mer, Riviera — Cote d'Azur

Welcome   Double with bath *$48-50*
1 quai Courbet   Telephone (93)552727

A perfectly glorious little place in which to end our trip through France. Right on sea near the old town, convenient to railway station and its *Saint-Pierre* restaurant, one of best in town for mixture of *haute cuisine* and Mediterranean provincial.

Markusturm / Rothenburg ob der Tauber

Germany

Germany, perhaps because it is so large, seems to group its attractions into little pockets or sharply defined regions. The Hansel-and-Gretel Black Forest, frolicsome Bavaria, the Rhine, Mosel, and Neckar River valleys with castles lining the banks and delightful villages in between, Rothenburg and the Romantic Road, and of course almost everyone's favorite German city, Munich. And just when one has written off central and northern Germany's rolling hills as infinitely forgettable, one chances upon a fetching little town in the Hartz Mountains, Celle with its storks or the beauty and vitality of Cologne and Hamburg.

Under a cloak of hard work and no nonsense, Germans are really romantics to the core. After all, this land of folklore and legend gave us the Brothers Grimm, Snow White, the Pied Piper of Hamlin, Baron Munchausen, Till Eulenspiegel and, more epic in nature, Siegfried, Lohengrin, the Nibelungen and Goethe's Faust. Beethoven, Brahms and Bach are but three peaks in a mountain range of composers spanning eight centuries. Today's German can be just as gregarious, fun-loving and fond of music as anyone on the Continent. At times he can be downright silly in his pursuit of a good time, as a day at *Oktoberfest* (Munich's or any small village's) will confirm.

Lufthansa, TWA, Pan Am, Delta and *Capitol* will get you there from the US; *Lufthansa* and *Air Canada* from Canada. *Lufthansa's* domestic network spans the country. *Avis, Hertz, Auto Sixt, Metro* and *Autourist* will rent you a VW *Polo* or Ford *Fiesta* for $180 a week unlimited mileage, plus 13% tax. Fuel is now about $2.00 per US gallon.

Deutsche Bundesbahn, the German Federal Railway, is close to the best on the Continent, honors *Eurailpass* and has a 9 and 16-day *GermanRail Tourist Card* at $165-215 and $120-155, first-class and second, respectively for the periods. Germany's bus system is part of the marvelous

Europabus network, offering numerous all-in tours, and information for rail and bus travel is available at German Federal Railroad offices in New York, Toronto and Houston, or from German National Tourist Offices in New York, Chicago, LA and Montreal.

The *deutsche mark* is Germany's currency, divided into 100 *pfennings*, and it's called *DM* or just plain *mark*. No matter what they're called, "How stands the *mark*?" is no longer a question. Just lay those traveler's checks on the nearest bank counter and you'll find it's worth about .40 or 2.5 to the dollar. Banking hours are 8:30-4:00, five days, and stores 9:00-6:00 for six. Voltage is 220, 50 cycles. Summer temperatures in Germany usually range in the 70s, winters in the nippy 30s.

Germans firmly believe that "meat is the best vegetable" and dining there is a carnivore's hereafter. The potato is king, game abundant, portions absolutely huge. If you doubt this, order a *bauernschmaus*, or farmer's feast, and get ready for a pork chop or two, one or more sausages, a slab of bacon, sauerkraut, potatoes and probably dumplings. German white wines are superior, a bit on the fruity side and the most popular are *Riesling, Silvaner* and *Muller-Thurgau*, a cross between the first two. Nobody brews beer like the Germans, light or dark, and we've been known to have it for breakfast in Munich with a *weisswurst* or two, glorious Munich mustard and coarse bread or a crisp *semmel* roll. *Himmlish!*

It's still possible to dine in *bierstube, gasthaus* or *schwemme* at reasonable cost, but in all truth German lodging and dining must be called moderate to expensive.

Hotels & Inns

Assmannshausen, 6220 Hessen (Rhine Valley)

Krone · Double with bath *$45-48*
Rheinstrasse 10 · Telephone (06722)2036

What started as a small inn in 1541 has grown steadily into one of the Rhine Valley's most charming hotels. Take your meals on terrace a few feet from barges on the river, drink Rhine and Mosel wines as well as a choice red from the hotel's own vineyards, then laze beside the pool and count your blessings. Near Mainz.

Auerbach, 8572 Bavaria

Goldner Lowe · Double with bath *$46-48*
Unterer Markt 9 · Telephone (09643)1765

Geranium boxes line the facade of this historic inn with every possible amenity, including a *Kegelbahn* in the cellar, so don't forget your bowling ball if you're a kegler.

Augsburg, 8900 Bavaria

Fischertor · Double with bath *$36-38*
Pfarrie 16 · Telephone (0821)30487

A small place with but 15 rooms in the Old Town behind Augsburg's massive cathedral. Very quiet and not far from railway station.

Baden-Baden, 7570 Baden-Wurttemberg

Gasthaus Auerhahn · Double with bath *$24-28*
Geroldsauer Strasse 160 · Telephone (07221)7435

Another modest one with only 11 rooms on the southern edge of this otherwise expensive spa. Hearty German food in restaurant.

Bamberg, 8600 Bavaria

Weinhaus Messerschmitt · Double with bath *$40-45*
Lange Strasse 41 · Telephone (0951)26471

By all means manage a visit to this medieval cathedral town on Regnitz River. Hotel a charmer and so is its restaurant, a local favorite managed by same family 150 years.

Berchtesgaden, 8240 Bavaria

Watzmann
Franziskanerplatz 6

Double with bath *$40*
Telephone (08652)2055

A longtime favorite and about as typically Bavarian as you can get. Antlers on every wall, window flower boxes and a spacious dining terrace for good food and sun, winter or summer.

Grassl
Maximilianstrasse 15

Double with bath *$46*
Telephone (08652)4071

Another older place, this one gone modern inside. On a gentle hill just above town, terrace dining again, sinful pastries.

Berlin, 1000

Pension Wittelsbach
31 Wittelsbachstrasse 22

Double with bath *$45*
Telephone (030)876345

Year after year readers praise this neat pension for its good food, small garden and thoughtful treatment of families with children. Small ones stay free.

Astoria
Berghausen 12
Fasanenstrasse 2

Double with bath *$50*
Telephone (030)3124067

Particularly convenient for rail arrivals as it's about 100 yards from station. Really inexpensive for rooms without baths here.

Remter
30 Marburger Strasse 17

Double with bath *$50*
Telephone (030)246061

Walking distance to *Kurfurstendamm,* Berlin's main thoroughfare, and other inner-city sights. All 32 rooms with baths.

Bischofswiesen, 8242 Bavaria

Pension Mooshausl   Double with bath *$38*
Jennerweg 11   Telephone (08652)7261

Near Berchtesgaden and a perfect spot for a few days layover for hiking or with children. Full pension rates very good.

Bonn, 5300 Nordrheim-Westfalen

Weiland   Double with bath *$40*
Breite Strasse 98a   Telephone (0228)652424

Seventeen sparkling rooms at this pleasant place in peaceful surroundings within old city. Garden, great for families.

Boppard am Rhein, 5407 Rhein

Rheinhotel zum Hirsch   Double with bath *$46*
Rheinallee 32   Telephone (06742)3041

Lots of *gemutlichkeit* inside and out, founded in 1520, dining on terrace beside Rhine and your own private balcony with same view. What more could one ask? Elegant service, typical fare.

Feuchtwangen, 8805 Bavaria

Greifen-Post   Double with bath *$42-58*
Marktplatz 8   Telephone (09852)2002

This lovely little town is but 17 miles south of Rothenburg and just as pretty. Hotel has been welcoming guests since 1588 with friendly service, good Franconian food and the finest wines.

Frankfurt am Main, 6000 Hessen

Excelsior Monopole   Double with bath *$52-56*
Mannheimer Strasse 7   Telephone (0611)230171

Probably most convenient location in town, across street from station. Huge rooms, some without baths at lower prices.

Freiburg, 7800 Baden-Wurttemberg

Zum Roten Baron   Double with bath *$45-60*
Oberlinden 12   Telephone (0761)36969

Said to be Germany's oldest inn, dating from the 12th century. In old city, has typical *Weinstube,* serves fine game dishes.

Garmisch-Partenkirchen, 8100 Bavaria

Posthotel Partenkirchen   Double with bath *$42-58*
Ludwigstrasse 49   Telephone (08821)51067

Here's the hotel to match this picture-postcard town, Bavarian rustic with excellent food and a good location near center.

Gasthof Fraundorfer   Double with bath *$42*
Ludwigstrasse 24   Telephone (08821)2176

A beautiful little place with Bavarian murals adorning its facade. More typical food and folk entertainment in the evenings.

Schneeferner Haus   Double with bath *$51*
Zugspitzplatt   Telephone (08821)58011

For the dedicated skier, hiker or climber, since it's perched only 900 feet below the summit of Germany's highest mountain. You must reach this one by cogwheel train or cable car, and the views are breathtaking from anywhere in the hotel.

Hamburg, 2000

Pension Irmgart Henk   Double with bath *$53*
Eilenau 24a, Hamburg 76   Telephone (040)252386

Marvel of a small, neat pension, kept to a high sparkle and just seven minutes to town center by underground. Frau Henk takes pride in her breakfasts, makes her own marmalades and you'll be happy!

Heidelberg, 6900 Baden-Wurttemberg
(see Hirschhorn)

Zum Pfalzgrafen   Double with bath *$37*
Kettengasse 21   Telephone (06221)20489

In the old city with most friendly owners, but it's also very modest and simple. Half of rooms have showers.

Zum Ritter   Double with bath *$40-70*
Hauptstrasse 178   Telephone (06221)20203

The High Renaissance facade of *Zum Ritter* stops just short of baroque and it's a marvel to behold. Lovliest of dining rooms is cozy yet sprays traditional atmosphere of old Heidelberg.

Hirschhorn, 6932 Hessen

Castle Hirschhorn   Double with bath *$42*
13 miles E of Heidelberg   Telephone (06272)1373

High above the Neckar River, this spectacular castle has overlooked valley since the 13th century. Outdoor dining terrace has stunning views down river. Exceptional food served well.

Jagsthausen, 7109 Baden-Wurttemberg

Burghotel Gotzenburg   Double with bath *$42*
18 miles NE of Heilbronn   Telephone (07943)2222
just off *autobahn*

Difficult to find, but well worth it, this 15th-century castle has been in the same family since then. A stately place with only 14 rooms. Food and wine are among region's very best.

Kronenburg-Dahlem, 5377 Nordrhein-Westfalen

Das Burghaus   Double with bath *$35*
Burgbering 4   Telephone (06557)265

A *Schlosshotel* mansion more than a century old set in gently rolling countryside practically on Belgian border north of Bitburg. Regal throughout, with dining to match, and a great value.

Munich, 8000 Bavaria

Wapler
2 Schwanthaler Strasse 8
Munich 2

Double with bath *$50-68*
Telephone (089)591664

Convenient to main railway station and a short walk to *Oktoberfest* grounds, this one is Bavarian traditional in both furnishings and feeling. Very peaceful, breakfast included and you'll love it.

Das Blaue Haus
Furstenstrasse 15
Munich 2

Double with bath *$40*
Telephone (089)281190

Huge rooms, the friendliest staff, a nice neighborhood of small shops and near *Odeonsplatz* underground station, but it's a brisk, 15-minute walk to city center. We've been happy here for years.

Schlicker
Tal 74
Munich 2

Double with bath *$44*
Telephone (089)227941

Perfect location just a step from *Marienplatz* and the city hall, and it's been an inn since 14th century. We like everything about it, but front desk hardly a paragon of friendly service.

Furst
Kardinal-Dopfner Strasse 8
Munich 2

Double with bath *$34-39*
Telephone (089)281043

A small pension one floor off street level very near *Das Blaue Haus* above. Modest, neat, and friendly people to help you.

Murrhardt, 7157 Baden-Wurttemberg

Sonne-Post
Karlsstrasse 6

Double with bath *$46-56*
Telephone (07192)8081

If business calls you to Stuttgart but the thought of staying there doesn't, try this 300-year-old post hotel, a half-hour's drive NE of town. Few places in Germany will feed you better.

Neckarzimmern, 6951 Baden-Wurttemberg

Burg Hornberg   Double with bath *$41-46*
27 miles SE Heidelburg   Telephone (06261)2758
on Neckar River

Standing tall in its vineyards, this regal but fortress-like hotel is justly proud of its restaurant. All 26 rooms with baths.

Nordlingen, 8860 Bavaria

Sonne   Double with bath *$33-48*
Marktplatz 3   Telephone (09081)5067

Dating from the 15th century, it's in a delightful medieval town where the nightwatchman still calls out the half-hour from 10 til midnight. Dead center of this perfectly preserved city.

Nurnberg, 8500 Bavaria

Weinhaus Steichele   Double with bath *$38-46*
Knorrstrasse 2   Telephone (0911)204378

A winehouse/hotel/restaurant that typifies everything we seek in an inn for our book: small, historic, beautifully decorated, superior food and a cloud of friendliness wafting throughout the place. Treat yourself to a visit or dinner here.

Victoria   Double with bath *$48*
Am Konigstor   Telephone (0911)203801

A most regal 19th-century hotel with rooms newly renovated into modern efficiency. Best location in town a step from main station and beside a charming Old Town village of cafes and shops displaying Nurnberg handicrafts.

Oberkirch, 7602 Baden-Wurttemberg

Obere Linde   Double with bath *$52*
Hauptstrasse 25   Telephone (07802)3038

Two unbelievably timbered buildings connected by a little

wooden bridge make up this colorful hotel of 46 rooms. The public areas are equally attractive, transporting you back to the inn's beginning in 1659. It's all character from lobby to roof.

Rastatt, 7550 Baden-Wurttemberg

Katzenberger's Adler   Double with bath *$36*
Josefstrasse 7   Telephone (07222)32103

Just east of the Rhine River at the north end of the Black Forest, this small place of only five rooms is noted more as a restaurant. Elegant, traditional and closed during July.

Ravensburg, 7980 Baden-Wurttemberg

Waldhorn   Double with bath *$49*
Marienplatz 15   Telephone (0751)23017

One of Ravensburg's oldest houses has been owned and run by the same family since 1860, probably because they run it so well. Superior food and service and Frau Bouley-Dressel insists on fresh flowers every day of the year, lilac in spring!

Rothenburg ob der Tauber, 8803 Bavaria

Markusturm   Double with bath *$45-60*
Rodergasse 1   Telephone (09861)2370

An inn since 1264, the *Markusturm* sits beside St. Mark's Tower (1204) and Roeder Arch (1330) in one of the most fetching towns of Germany's *Romantic Road*. Wooden walls, timber beams, art and handicrafts surround you in marvelous medieval hostelry.

Zur Glocke   Double with bath *$39-47*
Am Plonlein 1   Telephone (09861)3025

Just across from *Markusturm* on Rothenburg's most picturesque square, *Zur Glocke* is part of the same complex of medieval buildings. All the same atmosphere, plus a typical *weinstube* and *weinkeller* to liven up your stay.

Seigburg, 5200 Nordrhein-Westfalen

Siegblick

Nachtigallenweg 1

Double with bath *$35-39*

Telephone (02241)60077

A sparkling white country manor set in its own little forest beside pretty Sieg River, this lovely place is run by the Clarenz family with only their guests' well-being in mind. Neat, homey and the food is superb.

Spangenberg, 3509 Hessen

Schloss Spangenberg

24 miles SE of Kassel

Double with bath *$41-53*

Telephone (05663)866

Dating from 1214, the towers of this castle rise above a colorful village near the Fulda River. A full quota of turrets and moats go with the 24 rooms, fine food and wine. Game a specialty.

Uberlingen, 7770 Baden-Wurttemberg

Gasthof Grunen Baum

Double (no private baths) *$38*

Telephone (07551)3573

An ancient inn on the north shore of *Bodensee* (Lake Constance) where the attic rooms are delightful. The gracious owner once insisted that we join her for a nip of the local *schnapps* for breakfast. *Prost!*

Zell an der Mosel, 5583 Rheinland-Pfalz

Schloss Zell

Schloss Strasse 8

Double with bath *$55-65*

Telephone (06542)4084

You might expect longbow archers to launch arrows at you from the turrets of this 13th-century Gothic castle near the Mosel River. It's located 55 miles down a scenic road that follows the Mosel south from Coblenz, and consider yourself fortunate to book one of the 12 rooms. Obviously, the wine is glorious.

Aphrodite / Mykonos

Greece

Once your transportation has been paid to the far reaches of the Mediterranean, your wallet will enjoy Greece as much as you do. Here is the place to get even after all those chilly exchange rates in more northern climes. But more and more travelers are finding out about the warm sun and warmer reception in Greece, a good reason to consider late spring or September-October-November for your visit. Athens and the day-trips to Delphi and down the coast toward Sounion are of course a must, but don't hesitate to explore Macedonian Greece to the north, some of the less-popular smaller islands and, for the truly adventurous, Peloponnesos south of Corinth and Patras. Accommodations may be modest, but who needs the Ritz with blue water you could dip your pen in and write a letter with lapping at your bedroom window.

Olympia Airways and *TWA* will whisk you there from the US; *CP Air* from Toronto one stop to Athens. Ferry service from Brindisi, Italy will take you and your car at very moderate cost to Patras overnight, and *Olympic* has regular flights to many of the Greek Islands.

Greek currency is the *drachma*, currently 83 to the US dollar. *Hellascars, Avis, Hertz* and *Retca* will rent you a *Ford Fiesta* or *Fiat 127* for about $240 weekly with unlimited mileage, plus 18% tax, a rate that drops drastically for the large islands of Corfu, Crete and Rhodes, and for the period 1 November to mid-March. At this writing fuel is, alas, $2.35 per gallon and an International Driving License is required.

Hellenic Railways Organization (OSE) honors *Eurailpass* and has its own touring card good for 10, 20 and 30 days at 1750, 2900 and 3900 drachmas, current prices. This card may be purchased for up to five persons, with step price increases so that five travelers pay only 5200, 8600 and 11,700 *drachmas* for 10, 20 or 30 days, a real bargain. Bus travel costs in Greece, Aegean passenger ship fares between the islands and *Olympic Airways'* domestic route tickets are all tremendous values, just about the best in Europe.

Banking hours are from 9:00-3:00, six days, and store hours 9:00-2:00 and 4:30-8:00 p.m. Voltage is 220, 50 cycles. Summer temperatures are in the high 80s and 90s, winters average in the 40s and 50s, with the best months for a visit September through November.

Greek food is all gusto, fresh and invariably simplicity itself. Crisp salads laced with *feta* cheese and olive oil, seafood that has never seen a freezer, lamb to bring tears to your eyes and a chilled bottle of *retsina*, the resin flavored wine, to wash it all down with before Costa brings a very agreeable check. (Most Greek boys have a Constantine in their names, hence "Costa!" when you want just about anything from food to a taxi.)

Start with a *meze*, or appetizer, of *tzatziki*, a "dip" blended of cucumber, yogurt and garlic; *taramosalata*, another of carp roe, bread, mashed potatoes, lemon juice and onion or garlic; or *skordalia*, yet another of almost pure garlic, potatoes again and oil. Move on to *moussaka*, the baked dish of eggplant and ground meat; *souvlakia*, lamb grilled on a skewer; a bay-flavored, grilled swordfish steak or *barbounia*, the glorious red mullet that Greeks say no foreigner can eat properly due to the small bones. Perhaps add a side dish of salad; *dolmades*, rice-stuffed grape leaves; *spanakopita*, a spinach pie; or just nibble on olives with your main course.

Budget, bargain — whatever the word — Greece is it. Sheer delight for the visitor seeking value along with adventure, beauty and lively, hospitable people.

Hotels & Inns

Athens, (see also Glyfada, Old Phaliron, Kalamaki)

Adrian
74 Adrianou Street

Double with bath *$25*
Telephone (01)3221553

At the foot of the Acropolis in the Plaka, Athens' original settlement, this small place of 22 rooms has air-conditioning for the city's torrid days. Modest, simple, but it also has the obligatory rooftop restaurant with view of Parthenon.

Arethusa
6 Metropoleos Street

Double with bath *$32*
Telephone (01)3229431

A step from Constitution Square *(Syntagma)* in the heart of this bustling city. Stark contemporary, air-conditioned and another rooftop restaurant with breathtaking view of Acropolis by night or day, if Athens' notorious smog lifts.

Athenian Inn
22 Haritos Street
Kolonaki

Double with bath *$35*
Telephone (01)738097

This small pension, near Kolonaki Square below Lycabettos Hill, is a fairly recent and welcome addition. Very Greek in feeling with its stucco walls and typical furnishings, the inn is walking distance from the Benaki and Byzantine Museums where you'll find magnificent collections of Grecian art and icons.

Plaka	Double with bath *$29*
7 Kapnikareas Street	Telephone (01)3222096

A larger one we've watched for years, right in the Plaka and some rooms are air-conditioned. Has the usual roof garden and a typical Greek tavern such as you'll find throughout this colorful section.

Minerva	Double with bath *$31*
3 Stadiou Street	Telephone (01)3230915

Just off Constitution Square on the street leading up to Omonia Square, another city landmark. A bit hectic but comfortable. Most buses in Athens make a stop at Constitution Square.

Corfu, Ionian Islands

Arcadian	Double with bath *$34*
44 Kapodistriou	Telephone (0661)37672
Kerkyra (Corfu Town)	

Excellent location opposite huge park in the island's main town. Walking distance to ferry landing, shopping center, restaurants.

Avra	Double (no private baths) *$22*
Benitsa Village	Telephone (0661)29269

This tiny village lies beside a cobalt bay on the east shore of the island below Corfu Town. Inn is a few feet from water and prototype of small Greek hotels. Dining under an arbor. A simple place with few amenities. But many readers find it charming.

Crete

Xenia	Double with bath *$34*
S. Venizelou	Telephone (081)284000
Heraklion (Main City)	

Built as a project of the Greek National Tourist Office, *Xenia* hotels throughout Greece can usually be counted on for simple but clean and comfortable accommodations, even if they have been later sold to private firms. This one meets all the standards, including a restaurant. It also has a pool.

Old Corinth, Peloponese

Xenia Pavillon

Double with bath *$34*
Telephone (0741)31208

The good news is that *Xenia* is right across from the old ruins with a lovely garden of honeysuckle vines and pome-granate trees, plus excellent restaurant. The bad news is that there are only three rooms. Very little reason to stay in New Corinth.

Delphi, Central Greece

Xenia
Edge of Town

Double with bath *$38*
Telephone (0265)82151

Delphi's gods would have enjoyed the view from *Xenia's* garden overlooking the gorge below town toward the Sea of Corinth. Rooms simple but attractive and restaurant one of town's best.

Leto
25 Appolonos

Double with bath *$24*
Telephone (0265)82302

A small contemporary place with 22 rooms, air conditioning and a nice view also. Serves only breakfasts. We like it.

Glyfada, Attica

Antonopoulos
1 Vassilissia Friderikis

Double with bath *$34*
Telephone (01)8945636

Good location right on Aegean in this beach town near Athens. Has its own restaurant and there are lots of others nearby.

Ios, Cyclades Islands

Armadoros

Double with bath *$24*
Telephone (0286)91201

Just outside town but near beach on this lovely island. Has small restaurant and 27 rooms. Island ferry service sporadic.

Kalamaki, Attica

Galaxy
39 Vassileos Georgiou

Double with bath *$24*
Telephone (01)9818603

Another cool but hectic beach town seven miles from Athens. On the beach again, restaurant and many Greek taverns nearby.

Lesbos, Aegean Island

Xenia
1 mile from Mytilene

Double with bath *$35*
Telephone (0251)22713

Lesbos *(Lesvos)* is the third largest Greek island and one of the most popular. Choice of sparking beach or pool at *Xenia.*

Aghia Sion
In village of Aghiassos
15 miles SW of Mytilene

Double with bath *$18*
Telephone (0252)21358

Aghiassos, in the center of the island, is one of the most charming villages in Greece. Both the town and this small pension will transport you to the Greek Isles few ever see.

Mount Parnes, Attica

Xenia
20 miles N. of Athens

Double with bath *$24*
Telephone (01)2469101

On the mountain of the gods, a cool 3500 feet above Athens, you'll find this large and well-run hotel up in the pines. It's open only from June through September. Full restaurant.

Mykonos, Cyclades Islands

Aphroditi
7 miles east of Mykonos

Double with bath *$36*
Telephone (0289)71367

Nearly 100 bungalows that are more like mini-condos rising from their own beach on a blue gulf along the southern coast of the island. Pool, tennis, a few shops and lots of evening revelry at this one. Regular bus to and from Mykonos Town.

Theoxenia   Double with bath *$35*
On hill above town   Telephone (0289)22230

Spread across the top of a hill near the famous windmills, this one has a motel feeling but it's comfortable and quiet at night.

Andronikos   Double with bath *$30*
                                       Telephone (0289)22477

Small, family run pension is but 30 feet from the water. No meals here, but the harbor front has enough taverns to keep you fed during your stay.

Naxos, Cyclades Islands

Coronis   Double with bath *$24*
Paraliaki Leoforos   Telephone (0285)22626

You'll find everything you need on the largest and greenest of the Cyclades at this neat inn, including a rooftop restaurant.

Olympia, Peloponese

Xenia   Double with bath *$26*
14 miles W of town   Telephone (0624)22510
in Pirgos

Accommodations are sparse in Olympia and your best bet is in Pirgos, nearer the coast. Rooftop restaurant where the broiled red snapper is delicious. But then so is the roast lamb.

Patmos, Dodecanese Islands

Patmion   Double with bath *$24*
34 Emm. Xenou   Telephone (0247)31313

Best in town and just a few steps from the harbor, yet there is small beach in front. No restaurant but several at town center.

Old Phaliron, Attica

Aura
3 Nireos

Double with bath *$24*
Telephone (01)9814064

A most modest hotel for those days when you're really counting your *drachmas.* Not far from water but this is definitely not a beach hotel. Fine food at *Edem Restaurant* right on water and you'll hear *bouzouki* music, good and bad, at *tavernas* in beach towns and Plaka.

Rhodes, Dodecanese Islands

Spartalis
2 N. Plastira

Double with bath *$36*
Telephone (0241)24371

An old favorite of ours a block back from the harbor. Rooms with balconies overlook this spectacular bay and we're sure you'll like it, as most of our readers do.

Angela
7 October 28th Street

Double with bath *$36*
Telephone (0241)24614

Contemporary place, again with private balconies, in the center of town. Small restaurant here, but try *Manolis* in the old town where you'll enjoy the freshest seafood beneath shady trees on a tiny square.

Santorini, *(Thera)* Cyclades Islands

Panorama

Double with bath *$32*
Telephone (0268)22481

Both simple and spectacular at the same time, since your room looks across the bay 500 feet below. There's a small tavern with music in the evening, and the town itself is stunning. Local wine is not the earth's finest.

Selianitika, Peloponese

Kyani Akti

Double with bath *$22*
Telephone (0691)51202

Right on the Sea of Corinth and just off the old Patras-Corinth beach road, this typical place is a real find. Dining tables under shade trees at waters edge, excellent charcoal grilled fish and an authentic Greek tavern atmosphere.

Skiathos, Sporades Islands

Xenia
Town of Koukounaries

Double with bath *$32*
Telephone (0424)42041

On the southern coast of Skiathos you'll find this delightful town at water's edge and the *Xenia* to make your stay idyllic. On the dining terrace try the stuffed eggplant, a Greek specialty, or a beautifully prepared swordfish steak.

Skopelos, Sporades Islands

Aeolos

Double with bath *$25*
Telephone (0424)22233

A comfortable place on the edge of town, close to beach, no restaurant and charmingly decorated. You'll be happy here although newer places have sprung up with the island's growth. Lots of shady *tavernas* at water's edge in town with find food and flowing *retsina*.

Sounion, Attica

Surf (formerly Sun)
Pounta Zeza

Double with bath *$38*
Telephone (0292)22363

Some Greek hotels change names almost as often as they change spellings, but this one is still a hotel/bungalow complex, huge, with a big-resort feeling. Cape Sunion is almost a must for Athens visitors, if only to see the Temple of Poseidon crowning a hill at the southern tip of Attica.

Hortobagy Csarda / Hortobagy

Hungary

Budapest has always been known as the Paris of Central Europe and Hungary today is still the gayest of the Eastern-Bloc countries, has the best standard of living and somehow manages to take their Russian overseers with a grain of salt in the true Hungarian fashion. Hungary's red, white and green flag represents, according to Hungarians, the three types of paprika that lace their diet and give it more color than one usually sees on Central European tables. It is a beautiful country, particularly along the Danube River valley running due north-south from Czechoslovakia to Yugoslavia, and has a glorious playground in Lake Balaton, the largest inland lake in Europe.

Budapest is split by the Danube into the old city of Buda and the newer section of Pest. Both received horrible damages during World War II, laying waste the lovely old baroque buildings of the Austro-Hungarian Empire, but many have been rebuilt and today the city shines once again, usually well into the night as Hungarians are notorious cafe and coffee house patrons. They are also great horsemen, probably inherited from their Tartar forebears, and as indomitable in spirit as any people on the Continent. Budapest is only 160 miles from Vienna, a wondrous trip by Danube boat or hydrofoil, and surely once again it will become a must stop for those making the Grand Tour of Europe.

There are no direct flights from the US or Canada, but *MALEV*, the Hungarian airline, flies from major European capitals as do many other lines. Once there you may rent a *Lada 112* four-door or station wagon for $210 per week unlimited mileage, no tax, from *Avis* (through *IBUSZ*, the Hungarian travel bureau), *Volan, Fotaxi* or *Hertz*. An International Driver's License is required and super fuel about $2 per gallon.

Hungary does not honor *Eurailpass* but train travel is inexpensive and the country has its own discount pass. First-class fares are only about 2 cents per kilometer and longer runs are even less costly. Bus travel is about the same as first-class rail and longer-run, express buses are very good. There are also bus tours of the country and the *IBUSZ* office in New York has up-to-date information.

Hungary's currency is the *florint*, divided into 100 *filler*, and the current value in the US is .025 cents but, as with most Eastern Bloc countries, the rate is a bit higher there, around 3 cents. Banking hours are 9:00-3:00, five days, with stores open 10:00-6:00. Voltage is 220 and a visa is *definitely required* for travel within the country.

Hungary shares with France the reputation of being Europe's breadbasket, thanks to all that arable land, and Hungarians let none of it go to waste: they consume more per capita than any other Europeans. The cuisine is spicy, best typified by the Magyar dish goulash, and also leans heavily on the gypsy tradition of the violinist hovering over your table. (A gypsy recipe for an omelet begins: "First, steal three eggs...")

Pork is a staple and also the beef that Tartar horsemen once cured under their saddle blankets. You are likely to find the most typical dishes in a *czarda* wayside inn throughout the country, including *rablo-hus*, or robber's meat, skewered lamb, beef or pork served with pickles and potatoes. *Lesco* is a tomato and pepper ragout made noble by the addition of *Debreceni*, a Hungarian spicy sausage second to none in Europe, and *bourjuporkolt* is its veal stew counterpart. Hungarians are wine drinkers and Lake Balaton's shores produce excellent varieties. The sweet Tokay, however, is best ordered for dessert.

Hungary is a sensible and very satisfying destination for the budget-conscious traveler, with prices, as always, being lower outside large cities.

Hotels & Inns

Budapest

Astoria   Double with bath *$43*
1053 Kossuth Lajos utca 19   Telephone (1)173411

Fin de siecle Hapsburg atmosphere and furnishings at this mid-city hotel on Budapest's busiest street. Restaurant and grill, plus a great little Russian tea room, *Bajkal,* facing hotel.

Gellert   Double with bath *$64*
1111 Gallert ter 1   Telephone (1)460700

Very few members of European royalty have missed a stay at this Budapest fixture on banks of Danube. Thermal baths inside and the swimming pool has waves! Not the Grand Hotel it once was, but a visit here is a pleasant step backward in time.

Palace   Double with bath *$32*
1088 Rakoczi utca 43   Telephone (1)136000

Another older one in city center. Hungarian salami and cheese for breakfast, marvelous cold cherry soup at dinner, plus the usual gypsy music to help you enjoy the latter.

Buk

Kastely
9737 Buk

Double with bath *$24*
Telephone Buk 5

Not far from Austrian border you'll find this old baroque castle converted into pleasant hotel with large rooms and period furniture. Castle's annex is more modest, a bit cheaper.

Debrecen

Aranybika
4025 Voros Hadsereg utca 11

Double with bath *$28*
Telephone (52)16777

In eastern Hungary near Romanian border, this large town has one of the country's better hotels. Area noted for cattle and city famous for *Debrecena wurst,* a peppery marvel we love.

Eger

Eger
3300 Szalloda utca 1

Double with bath *$28*
Telephone (36)13233

About 60 miles northeast of Budapest you'll find one of the country's most classically beautiful towns on edge of huge and lovely Bukki Nemzeti Park. *Eger* has newer twin nearby.

Esztergom

Furdo
2500 Bajcsy Zs. utca 14

Double with bath *$20*
Telephone Esztergom 147

This spa town, on banks of Danube as it leaves Czech border for Budapest, makes nice day-trip from capital. If you decide on overnight, the *Furdo* offers most of the amenities at good price.

Gyongyos

Matra
3200 Matyas kir. utca 2

Double with bath *$28*
Telephone (37)12057

Also northeast of Budapest about 33 miles, Gyongyos lies near Matra Hills that furnish fresh game for the hotel's tables. A stately building, made gayer by its lively folklore murals.

Hortobagy

Hortobagy Csarda   Double with bath *$15*
4071 Hortobagy   Telephone Hortobagy 17

Right in the middle of another lovely Hungarian national park, this 200-year-old inn was once a bank of riding stables. Now it's primarily a restaurant, but keeps a few rooms still. Inn and restaurant both rustic studies in old peasant furnishings.

Sarospatak

Borostyan   Double with bath *$16*
3950 Kadar K. utca 28   Telephone Sarospatak 164

On Hungary's northeast Czech border near Russia, you'll find this modest place beside a 16th-century monastery/castle. Just 13 rooms, with restaurant in cellar of monastery.

Siofok (Lake Balaton)

Venus   Double with bath *$24*
8600 Kinizsi utca 12   Telephone (84)10660

Many hotels on Balaton quote room prices with full-board. The Venus quotes about $40 for two during high season. Most rooms have balconies and there's a rooftop terrace and solarium.

Europa   Double with bath *$26*
8600 Petofi setany 15   Telephone (84)11400

Much larger than *Venus* and a notch up in class. Restaurant, rooftop bar, tennis courts, private beach, everything you could want.

Sopron

Palatinus   Double with bath *$24*
9400 Uj utca 23   Telephone (99)11395

On Austrian border 40 miles south of Vienna, this classic

medieval town is filled with historic monuments and has several interesting castles within a short drive. Hotel new in 1981, good value.

Szeged

Tisza
6701 Wesselenyi utca 1

Double with bath *$28*
Telephone (62)12466

Szeged is on southern border near Yugoslav-Romanian frontier and it's the paprika capital of the universe, so ask for them with scrambled eggs in the morning. Delicious!

Szolnok

Tisza
5000 Marx Park 2

Double with bath *$26*
Telephone (56)12222

Facade of hotel has rather ecclesiastic look, but within it offers everything, including its own thermal baths. Best in this Tisza River city noted for curative spas.

Tata

Diana
2890 Remetesegpuszta

Double with bath *$34*
Telephone Tata 715

An old castle in Remetesegpuszta Forest about 2½ miles from Tata. Town near Danube on Czech border and it's an equestrian center in country that idolizes horsemanship. Fine wine cellar.

Tihany (Lake Balaton)

Kistihany
8237 Tihany

Double with bath *$28*
Telephone(80)44011

Town on peninsula that juts down from northern shore of Balaton, Hungary's favorite playground. All 20 rooms have baths and balconies. Your own private beach, restaurant nearby.

John Barleycorn / Cork

Ireland

Ireland is a breathtaking land of almost fierce beauty. Unbelievably green even when you expected an Emerald Isle, the rolling glens, lush meadows and peat-covered bogs still take your senses unawares. Mountains reach out like fingers into the wild Atlantic to create majestic bays all along the western and southern coasts. And the secluded valleys, lakes and rivers of the interior counties are no less appealing to the eye and spirit. The weather too can take you unawares, changing from cloud-fleeced sky to the chill wet lash of a morning storm with all the swiftness of a legendary leprechaun.

The people are a warm, friendly lot, full of charm, kindness, a bit of blarney and perhaps a Guinness or two. They love conversation, weighty or otherwise, but much prefer to spin a dark or winsome tale of the imagination rather than a dull one fettered with facts. While the English may be slow to warm to conversation, God knows you'll hear enough from any Irishman within earshot.

Aer Lingus, Northwest and *Transamerica* will fly you there from the US, *Air Canada* from Canada. *Murrays, Dan Ryan, Cahill's, Hertz* and *Avis* are car hire firms and they will rent you a Ford *Fiesta* or *Escort* for around $200 per week unlimited mileage, plus 10% tax. Fuel for it will cost about $3.20 per US gallon. *CIE* is the Irish railway and bus system, and an excellent one it is. *Eurailpass* is now honored in Ireland and there is a *CIE Rambler Ticket* for eight or 15 days, either rail or rail-and-bus, at moderate cost. Rail for eight days is $62, rail-bus $76, with children half that. A 15-day adult *Rambler* is $88 rail, $109 rail-bus. A real bargain.

The Irish pound is currently $1.33, which makes the dollar worth 75 pence. Banking hours are 10:00-12:30, 1:30-3:00 for five days. Stores 9:00-6:00, six days. Voltage is 220, 50 cycles.

Irish food is a great deal like Britain's, including monumental breakfasts. Beef, lamb and mutton are excellent, even when buried in a stew, and Limrick ham is famous. Galway Bay oysters are among the best in the world and Dublin Bay prawns grace the tables of Europe's finest restaurants. Ireland's Monday night special, bacon and cabbage with enough mashed potatoes to hold you until Wednesday, somehow seems best when ordered in a pub or modest restaurant with a pint of beer or Guinness stout. And Irish soda bread, all warm and mouth-watering, is surely one of the most heavenly breads on earth, whether baked in an oven or over the traditional peat fire.

Potatoes continue to make up a good part of the Irish diet and these "praties" are made into a pancake or "boxty," also mashed with chopped scallions and fresh butter for a main course known variously as "thump," "stelk" or "champ."

No mention of Ireland is complete without an ode to Irish whiskey, always spelled with an "e" and true nectar when taken by the "splash" or "jar" amid a sea of Irish faces in the nearest pub. Pubs, incidentally, are far more modest than those of England, save a few that have been tarted up in Dublin, but they are also even more of a social center than in Britain and practically classless. The hod carrier chats with the bank president, probably about horses, and it's a great place to make friends.

Ireland, from a neat farmhouse in County Clare to Dublin's finest restaurants, is a country you will feel immediately at home in. And by any scale its prices are budget, a bargain and a boon to its fortunate visitors.

Hotels & Inns
(Bed and Breakfast)

Bansha, Tipperary

Bansha House   Double (no private baths) *$22*
5 miles SE of Tipperary   Telephone (062)54194

No private baths, but this delightful Georgian farm won recent best-in-region award. Dinner served, free pony rides for kids.

Blarney, Cork

Birch Hill House, Grenagh   Double (no private baths) *$22*
4 miles from Blarney   Telephone (021)886106

More than a century old, this Victorian manor is set in 100-plus wooded acres. A working farm, high teas and dinner, trout fishing.

Caragh Lake, Kerry

Caragh Lodge
On lake near Glenbeigh

Double with bath *$45*
Telephone Caragh Lake 15

A German couple has created the perfect retreat, all coziness and tropical gardens, fine food, boats for fishing on lake and set in a ten-acre estate. Very popular so book or call early.

Cashel Bay, Galway

Cashel House
Head of Cashel Bay

Double with bath *$58*
Telephone Cashel 9

Formerly a stately home on the rugged and beautiful Connemara Coast east of Galway, this 23-room hotel received a two-week visit from General and Madame De Gaulle shortly after opening. Dinners are noteworthy and, again, it's a very popular place.

Castledermot, Kildare

Kilkea Castle
40 miles S of Dublin

Double with bath *$58*
Telephone (0503)45156

Normans built it in 1180 and it's the oldest in-service castle in Ireland. All 55 rooms have baths, heated swimming pool, hunting and fishing in the area. You'll feel like royalty, at least!

Clifden, Galway

Rock Glen Country House

Double with bath *$44*
Telephone Clifden 16

Another of our longtime favorites on the wild and scenic Connemara Coast, this one a former hunting lodge with glorious Irish food.

Cork, Cork

John Barleycorn
4 miles from Cork City
at Rivertown, Glanmire

Double with bath *$46*
Telephone (021)821499

An 18th-century former residence just off Cork-Dublin road

that still has the charm of an old coaching stop right out of Dickens.

Arbutus Lodge
Montenotte hill in suburbs

Double with bath *$60*
Telephone (021)501237

Through the years we've watched the *Arbutus* grow from a simple guest house into an outstanding inn noted throughout Ireland/Britain for its marvelous food and wine list. Only 20 rooms, all with baths.

Ashford House
Donovan's Road

Double (no private baths) *$20*
Telephone (021)263241

Another old standby, this one a town house B&B directly opposite Cork University campus. Their high teas were marvelous.

Dublin

Ariel House
52 Lansdowne Road,
Ballsbridge, Dublin 4

Double with bath *$36*
Telephone (01)685512

A high-stooped Victorian just south of city center that draws unbridled raves from readers. All 16 rooms have private baths.

Egan's House
7 Iona Park,
Glasnevin, Dublin 9

Double with bath *$32*
Telephone (01)303611

Very comfortable, family run guesthouse in north section of city, convenient to Dublin airport. Evening meal served here.

North Star
Amiens Street
Dublin 1

Double with bath *$55*
Telephone (01)741136

Just across from railway station and very much a mid-city hotel, but it's well run, serves all meals and certainly convenient.

Dundrum, Tipperary

Dundrum House
7 miles W of Cashel

Double with bath *$40*
Telephone (062)71116

An 18th-century Georgian manor house with every possible amenity and activity for an extended stay. Fishing or horseback riding right on the 100-acre estate. Delightful meals and wine list.

Ennis, Clare

Newpark House
Mile E of Ennis
off Tulla road

Double (no private baths) *$25*
Telephone (065)21233

One of the loveliest farmhouses you'll ever see, 300 years old and set on 85 acres. Evening meal served, only seven rooms.

Foulksmills, Wexford

Mill House
12 miles E of Wexford

Double (no private baths) *$25*
Telephone (051)63683

A vine-covered Georgian farmhouse named for its water-powered mill, with only five rooms but marvelous Irish cooking.

Galway, Galway

Skeffington Arms
Eyre Square

Double with bath *$45*
Telephone (091)63173

Right in the center of this popular city for exploring the Connemara Coast and west of Ireland. Eyre a lively market square and you'll find Galway Bay oysters on the half shell at the nearby fish market. Only 21 rooms but full meal service.

American
Eyre Square

Double with bath *$38*
Telephone (091)62245

Another small one in the center, but very few rooms with private baths. *Cladagh Restaurant* in *Great Southern Hotel* town's finest, but *Paddy Burke's Pub* on Dublin road your best bet for Galway oysters.

Banba   Double with bath *$38*
Salthill resort
E of Galway   Telephone (091)21944

The charm of this Galway Bay resort has always eluded us, but the *Banba* has 30 comfortable rooms (two with baths) and full dining service. Hotel fronts the bay.

Gort, Galway

Glynn's   Double with bath *$54*
Center of town   Telephone Gort 27

A little vine-covered charmer in pleasant town on Ennis-Galway road. Excellent food and altogether a delight.

Innishannon, Cork

Innishannon Hotel   Double with bath *$40*
16 miles SW of Cork
near Bandon   Telephone (021)75121

This marvel of an 18th-century estate is spread along the scenic riverfront above Kinsale Harbor, has 13 rooms with baths and is noted far and wide for its dining room. Plan a short stay for fishing, walking or just enjoying the bucolic setting.

Kanturk, Cork

Assolas Country House   Double with bath *$45*
30 miles E of Killarney
off N72   Telephone Kanturk 15

Another magnificent 18th-century estate, vine-covered, rather formal and surrounded by award-winning gardens. Facing a tranquil little river right off a travel poster. Family run and wonderful.

Kenmare, Kerry

Templenoe House, Greenane Double (no private baths) *$24*
4 miles from Kenmare   Telephone (064)41538
on Kenmare Bay

Lovely old dairy farm at head of Kenmare Bay on renowned

Ring of Kerry. Our readers love this one, but be sure to book ahead as there are only five rooms. Fine evening meal served.

Killaloe, Clare

Lakeside Hotel
13 miles NE of Limerick

Double with bath *$50*
Telephone (061)76122

This neat hotel is right on banks of River Shannon below Lough Derg, a half-hour from Shannon Airport. Set in rolling hills amid spectacular scenery, it offers substantial discounts for children, as do most farms and guest houses in Ireland.

Killarney, Kerry

Arbutus
Center of town

Double with bath *$37*
Telephone (064)31037

Family run with one of best restaurants in town. Killarney usually crowded beyond belief in mid-summer, so book ahead.

Scott's
Center of town

Double with bath *$47*
Telephone (064)31060

Another modest small hotel, but we've always enjoyed it and the full Irish breakfasts are superb. Few private baths.

Kinsale, Cork

Murphy's Farm House
1 mile from Kinsale
off Cork road

Double (no private baths) *$25*
Telephone (021)72229

This four-room farmhouse near one of Ireland's most picturesque seaport towns is a sensible place to put up for a few days. Mrs. Murphy's evening meals are all solid Irish fare.

Limerick, Limerick

Woodfield House
Ennis Road

Double with bath *$36*
Telephone (061)53023

We discovered this cozy place while escaping the less-than-inviting bustle and clutter of mid-city Limerick. Most of the

25 rooms have private baths and the warm atmosphere of public rooms give the *Woodfield* an overall feeling of well-being.

Listowel, Kerry

Listowel Arms   Double with bath *$45*
Town center   Telephone (068)21500

A lovely old Georgian place on small square in typical Irish market town. Superior food and don't miss a visit to huge Market Square.

Macroom, Cork

Castle   Double with bath *$32*
Main Street   Telephone Macroom 74

Another find, particularly for its dining room that is so popular you may have to queue up for lunch with the locals. Same family owns Killarney's *Arbutus* and we like both of them.

Rathkeal, Limerick

Smithfield House, Croagh   Double (no private baths) *$24*
3 miles NE of Rathkeal   Telephone (069)64114

This 200-year-old Georgian house is just off Killarney-Limerick road and it's a budget haven if one of the three rooms is available. A 100-acre dairy farm with sturdy farm-house evening meal.

Rathnew, Wicklow

Hunter's Hotel   Double with bath *$45*
1 mile N of town   Telephone (0404)4106
on L29

One of Ireland's oldest coaching stops on the coastal road along the Irish Sea 30 miles south of Dublin. Excellent seafood in dining room as well as fresh vegetables from hotel garden.

Sixmilebridge, Clare

County Guesthouse   Double (no private baths) *$24*
Main Street   Telephone (061)72119

A very modest house in village as picturesque as its name.
Just six miles from Shannon Airport and four from colorful
evening banquets at *Knappogue* and *Bunratty* castles, both
most worthy.

Tralee, Kerry

Benner's   Double with bath *$46*
Town center   Telephone (066)21422

A fine older hotel with excellent dining room, cozy bar and
comfortable furnishings. Town terribly crowded during fall
Festival of Kerry. It's also a crafts center where carders,
spinners, weavers and potters practice their ancient skills
and display work in Tralee's shops year-round.

Sole al Pantheon / Rome

Italy

Italy is still the dream destination most romantics seek. Art, architecture, stunning scenery and coastlines, music, lively citizens, some of the best and most varied dining in Europe, great wines and cheeses, color, tempo, good accommodations in all categories, excellent roads and a fine transportation system, when it's not on strike!

Visitors with limited budgets would do well to vacate Rome-Venice-Florence after the obligatory few days and head for the less-known south, Adriatic coast, Sicily, Sardinia and regions like Abruzzi, Umbria and Val d'Aosta. And, as always, shun the big cities if your wallet is thin. The Big Three are of course a must, but you'll find fewer of your peers in the small towns and villages, which is always a blessing.

Summer temperatures in most of the country cling in the 80s and 90s, mountains being the exception. While winters are mild in the south, they are often bone-chilling from Florence north. Rule of summer dress in Southern Europe: cottons are coolest, synthetics loathesome.

Alitalia, TWA and *Pan Am* will get you to Italy from the US; *Alitalia* and *CP Air* from Canada. *Alitalia, ATI, Itavia* and *Alisarda* are domestic lines and don't fail to check *Alitalia's* tours and excursion rates — they're tempting. *Maggiore, Avis, Hertz, Europacar* and *Majellano* are car rental firms and a *Fiat 127* will cost you about $256 per week with unlimited mileage, a roomier *128* about $285, with 18% tax tacked on to both. "Super" fuel will cost you 1020 *lire* per liter, or about $2.77 per gallon, but both *Fiats* above will average 35 + mpg road driving for a reasonable cost of eight cents per mile.

Italian State Railways, with offices in New York, Chicago, LA, Toronto and Montreal, honor *Eurailpass* and have their own *BTLC Italian Tourist Ticket*. Buy them in Italy for 8, 15, 21 or 30 days and the cost for those periods is (first-class) $114, 139, 166 and 202; (second-class) $72, 87, 102 and 127. A fine bus system operates throughout Italy and the islands, with fares about the same as first-class rail travel.

The *lira* is Italy's currency and it's currently worth about .0007 or 1428 *lire* to the dollar. Write out a small card for your wallet with the dollar value for 100, 500, 1000, 5000 and 10,000 *lire* as soon as you arrive. That way you won't tip $3.50 when you had 35 cents in mind. Banking hours are 9:30-2:00, Monday-Friday, with store hours varying. In the south the noon break is longer and stores frequently stay open until 7:00 or 8:00 p.m. Electric current can be 115 or 220 volts.

Almost everybody thinks they know Italian cooking and, unless they've been to Italy, usually don't. Far from being mounds of *pasta* under mounds of tomato sauce, Italian menus will offer you a greater selection of tempting dishes than any cuisine save French and perhaps Chinese. Marvelous steaks in Tuscany, veal like you wish you could afford at home, pork, game and seafood just hours from the net. Rice and *pasta* are prepared in more ways than you can imagine and any Italian cook would rather turn in his spatula than dare serve frozen vegetables. Desserts are downright sinful!

Wines you are sure to enjoy are the regal *Barolo*, classic *Chianti* (each vineyard in Tuscany has its specialty), *Soave, Valpolicella, Bardolino, Pinot Grigio, Orvieto, Verdicchio* and the crisp *Ischia*. Most Italian cheeses are found throughout the country, but vary in subtlety from province to province. The same with salami, although subtle is probably not the word.

We rate Italy a medium-priced country on just about any scale, with dining probably one of Europe's outstanding budget values. And if you don't find yourself in an instant love affair with the country and its people, then I'm afraid you're very much the exception.

Hotels & Inns

Agrigento, 92100 Sicily

Della Valle
Via dei Templi 94

Double with bath *$33*
Telephone (0922)26966

View town's magnificent Grecian temples from your window, then enjoy memorable Sicilian pasta in hotel dining room.

Jolly dei Templi
SS 115

Double with bath *$40*
Telephone (0922)76144

Every convenience including a pool, plus the fine buffet breakfasts you'll find in *Jolly* hotels throughout Italy.

Alghero, 07041 Sardinia

Villa Las Tronas
Lungomare 1

Double with bath *$54*
Telephone (0791)975390

Former summer residence of Italian royal family and still looks it. Private beach, pool, superior food and service. Excellent rooms in nearby annex for about 20% less.

Amalfi, 84011 Campania

Caleidoscopio
Lone district, outskirts

Double with bath *$32*
Telephone (089)871220

Escape mid-summer Amalfi hordes at this hilltop haven with great view, pool, lots of flowers and commendable dining.

Arabba, 32020 Veneto (Dolomites)

Pordoi
Hamlet 22 miles W. of Cortina

Double with bath *$26*
Telephone (0436)79113

Family style chalet in fetching village at base of Marmolada Mountains. Cowbells tinkle, wildflowers galore, most bucolic!

Assisi, 06081 Umbria

Subasio
Via Frate Elia 2

Double with bath *$36*
Telephone (075)812206

Marvelous older hotel right beside Basilica of St. Francis. Endless array of terrace rooms overlook gentle Umbrian hills.

Umbra
Vicolo degli Archi 6

Double with bath *$34*
Telephone (075)812240

Finest dining and wine list in town and the roast pigeon stuffed with truffles a marvel. Convenient to main piazza.

Europa
Via Metastasio 2

Double with bath *$26*
Telephone (075)812412

A bit more modest than the two above, but the parklike surroundings are lovely and it's near everything in town.

Bassano del Grappa, Veneto

| Belvedere | Double with bath *$40* |
| Piazzale Generale Giardino 14 | Telephone (0424)29845 |

Another superior dining room awaits you in this pleasant gateway city to the Dolomites and the same family owns rustic *Taverna de Marostega* just four miles from town.

Baveno, 28042 Piedmont (Lake Maggiore)

| Eden | Double with bath *$32* |
| Viale Vittori | Telephone (0323)24560 |

Modest but comfortable old favorite on main piazza of this lovely lakeside town just two miles from Stresa.

| Simplon | Double with bath *$41* |
| Viale Vittoria | Telephone (0323)24112 |

Also on street fronting lake and a notch up in class with colorful gardens, tennis court and nice pool.

Bellagio, 22021 Lombardy (Lake Como)

| Excelsior Splendide | Double with bath *$36* |
| Heart of town on lake | Telephone (031)950225 |

Regal public rooms filled with antiques, dining under arbor in delightful garden beside lake, very Italian.

Belluno/Nevegal, 32024 Veneto

| Nevegal | Double with bath *$33* |
| Seven miles from Belluno | Telephone (0437)98141 |

This summer-winter resort lodge in mountains high above Belluno serves spectacular food on its pension plan.

Bologna, 40100 Emilia-Romagna

| Tre Vecchi | Double with bath *$32* |
| Via Indipendenza 47 40121 | Telephone (051)231991 |

An old standby convenient to everything in the heart of this bustling city. Dining not quite up to local fare.

Regina   Double with bath *$30*
Via Indipendensa 51 40121   Telephone (051)236817

A few steps away from *Tre Vecchi* you'll find this one. No dining room here but area filled with restaurants.

Bolsena, 01023 Lazio

Le Naiadi   Double with bath *$26*
On Lake Bolsena   Telephone (0761)98017

Very much like a private club with own beach right on lake. Lots of family activity and a super kitchen.

Bolzano, 39100 Trentino/Alto Adige

Figl   Double with bath *$32*
Piazza del Grano 9   Telephone (0471)21412

A typical *gasthof* reflecting the region's Germanic flavor. The Italo-Austrian menu one of town's best.

Bressanone, 39042 Trentino/Alto Adige

Elefante   Double with bath *$50*
Via Rio Bianco 4   Telephone (0472)22288

Famous with epicures throughout Europe for its classic dining, sumptous accommodations and lovely setting.

Cagliari, 09100 Sardinia

Jolly   Double with bath *$38-46*
Viale Regina Margherita 44   Telephone (070)651971

Best location in Cagliari, near the port and colorful Via Roma evening promenade. Don't miss city museum.

Campotosto, 67013 Abruzzi

Valle   Double with bath *$28*
On Lake Campotosto   Telephone (0862)900119

A neat little chalet run by Luciano Deli and his family with fanatical attention to service and glorious food.

Canazei, 38030 Trentino/Alto Adige (Dolomites)

Stella Alpina   Double with bath *$28*
Heart of village   Telephone (0462)61127

Another fetching chalet with gingerbread architecture, geranium boxes, babbling brook nearby, fine kitchen.

Capri, 80073 Campania

Belvedere e Tre Re   Double with bath *$32*
Marina Grande   Telephone (081)8370345

Shun the summertime crowds in peaceful garden setting just a mile from the main village. Charming!

Catanzaro, 88100 Calabria

Grand   Double with bath *$40*
Piazza Matteotti   Telephone (0961)25605

Why not the best in this colorful Ionian Sea coastal city? Perfect central location, modern, a nice change.

Cefalu, 90015 Sicily

Artu   Double with bath *$31*
SS 113   Telephone (0921)21450

Off the beach in popular resort, but close to town center. Comfort and prices make up for location.

Certaldo, 50052 Tuscany

Osteria del Vicario   Double (no private baths) *$26*
Town center   Telephone (0571)668228

This 13th-century villa in our favorite Tuscan hill town might be the highlight of your trip. Book ahead!

Cervinia, 11021 (Valtournenche), Valle D'Aosta

Les Neiges D'Antan   Double with bath *$34*
Main road just below town   Telephone (0166)948775

Typical *valdostana* mountain inn in renowned winter-summer playground. Kitchen one of finest in all Italy.

Como, 22100 Lombardy

Terminus
Lungo Lario Trieste 14

Double (no private baths) *$32*
Telephone (031)267042

Marble palace right on lakefront with small garden and bar. Indeed, has everything but dining, private baths.

Cortina d'Ampezzo, 32043 Veneto (Dolomites)

Colombia
Via Ronco 14

Double with bath *$34*
Telephone (0436)3607

A neat chalet on hill above town with spectacular view of valley. Breakfast only but see note below.

Villa Neveda
Via Ronco 64

Double with bath *$34*
Telephone (0436)4778

Another sparkling chalet not far from ski lifts. Also no dining but try food at nearby *Da Beppe Sello.*

Courmayeur, 11013 Valle D'Aosta

Chalet Chanton
Hamlet of Entreves

Double (no private baths) *$26*
Telephone (0165)89913

Modest pension with sunny Mont Blanc through your window and steps to glorious *Maison de Filipo* food.

Erice, 91016 Sicily

Moderno
Via Vittorio Emanuele

Double with bath *$32*
Telephone (0923)869300

Your best bet in this spectacular and cool mountaintop town high above Sicily's western coast.

Florence, 50123 Tuscany

Balestri
Piazza Mentana 7
50122 Florence

Double with bath *$52*
Telephone (055)214743

This family owned hotel, beside Arno River just steps from Ponte Vecchio and Uffizi Gallery, our 25-year favorite.

Aprile   Double with bath *$42*
Via della Scala 6   Telephone (055)216237
50123 Florence

Half of Florence's hotels seem to be historic; this little gem near railway station a 15th-century Medici palace.

Berchielli   Double with bath *$59*
Lungarno Acciaioli 14   Telephone (055)211530
50123 Florence

Another late Renaissance palace that we first visited in the 50s. On Arno and all charm from lobby to roof.

Pension Hermitage   Double with bath *$41*
Vicola Marzio 1   Telephone (055)287216
50123 Florence

Dead center of Florence where you can reach anything afoot or see most of it from rooftop garden. 14 rooms.

Frascati, 00044 Lazio

Bellavista   Double with bath *$28*
Piazza Roma 2   Telephone (06)9421068

Delightful hill town overlooking Rome just off *autostrada*. Frascati noted for its wine and exceptional dining.

Genoa, 16136 Liguria

Milano Terminus   Double with bath *$36*
Via Balbi 34 16136   Telephone (010)262264

An old standby convenient to railway station and port with its galaxy of small but good seafood restaurants.

La Capannina   Double with bath *$34*
Via Tito Speri 7 16146   Telephone (010)363205

A small one in the Boccadasse beach area east of city. Own good restaurant with clutch of others nearby.

Gubbio, 06024 Umbria

Bosone   Double with bath *$36*
Via XX Setembre 22   Telephone (075)923008

An old palace made modern in fascinating Umbrian town. Take meals in same owner's glorious *Taverna del Lupo*.

Limone, 25010 Lombardy (Lago di Garda)

Lido	Double with bath *$34*
On Lake Garda	Telephone (0365)954100

Limone is on the precipitous, shady side of Garda, often called the "British" side. Still, lots of lovely sun.

Madonna di Campiglio, 38084 Trentino-Alto Adige

Norma	Double with bath *$35*
Edge of town	Telephone (0465)41110

Discover one of Italy's best kept secrets in this ski/summer resort near Trento. Norma a neat small pension.

Matera, 75100 Basilicata

President	Double with bath *$36*
Via Roma 113	Telephone (0835)214075

Former member of *Jolly* chain dead center of a most fascinating city. A few natives still living in caves.

Mestre, 30170 Veneto

Alla Giustizia	Double with bath *$36*
Via Miranese 111	Telephone (041)931955

Just across causeway from Venice, with much friendlier prices, and probably the best seafood table in town.

Milano, 20100 Lombardy

Gran Duca di York	Double with bath *$42*
Via Moneta 1-A 20123	Telephone (02)874863

In a medieval building and a short walk from Cathedral, La Scala and the Galleria, Milano's lively living room.

Ariston	Double with bath *$42*
Largo Carrobbio 2 20123	Telephone (02)8057293

What it lacks in Old World charm it makes up for in comfort and convenient, central-city location.

Naples, 80100 Campania

Britannique   Double with bath *$43*
Corso Vittorio Emanuele 133   Telephone (081)660933

This Siamese-twin sister of the first-class *Parker's* beside it
has fine view of the bay and good kitchen.

Parker's   Double with bath *$50*
Corso Vittorio Emanuele 135   Telephone (081)684866

Naples' oldest but a bit removed from the hectic *conbrio* life
of the city, a blessing you may cherish.

Naturno, 39025 Trentino-Alto Adige

Castello   Double with bath *$32*
                                     Telephone (0473)39025

A 13th-century castle in delightful village just 9 miles west of
Merano. Great mountain views, food.

Nuoro, 08100 Sardinia

Fratelli Sacchi   Double with bath *$40*
On Monte Ortobene   Telephone (0784)31200

Short drive high above Sardinia's most typical city brings
you to this charmer with incredible dining.

Oliena, 08028 Sardinia

Su Gologone   Double with bath *$32*
Five miles from Oliana   Telephone (0784)287512

The very essence of Sardinia in a mad ramble of limestone
buildings brimming with antiques, local handicrafts, original
paintings and authentic island food roasting away over
aromatic wood in a gigantic fireplace.

Ortisei, 39046 Trentino-Alto Adige (Dolomites)

Regina   Double with bath *$36*
                                     Telephone (0471)76329

Gateway village to glorious Val Gardana and teeming with

skiers or climbers. This perfect pension has everything, plus flowers!

Ostuni, 72017 Puglia

Incanto   Double with bath *$40*
Via dei Colli   Telephone (0831)971781

Delightful hill town on heel of Italy's boot with view of coast and Albania! Elegant *Incanto* graces another hill outside town.

Palermo, 90100 Sicily

Touring   Double with bath *$31*
Via Stabile 126 90141   Telephone (091)584444

Dead center of this great lush melon of a city with lots of shops and restaurants nearby. Hotel small but adequate.

Ligurai   Double with bath *$33*
Via Stabile 128 90100   Telephone (091)581588

A step away from *Touring* above and even smaller, but the price is right for both. Less expensive rooms here with no baths.

Parma, 43100 Emilia-Romagna

Button   Double with bath *$34*
Via San Vitale 7   Telephone (0521)33177

Small wonder of a hotel a step away from *Farini's,* where Verdi lovers gather for some of best food in all Northern Italy.

Perugia, 06100 Umbria

La Rosetta   Double with bath *$41*
Piazza Italia 19   Telephone (075)20841

Heart of this gorgeous Umbrian city but dining in the heavenly garden patio may make your forget your surroundings.

Minerva   Double with bath *$28*
Via C. Caporali 9   Telephone (075)61128

Small and modest with only 13 rooms but the dining room is very good along with the price and location. We like it.

Petralia Sottana, 90027 Sicily

Pomieri   Double with bath *$26*
Mid-village   Telephone (0921)41189

Find the real Sicily in this tiny hill town just off Palermo-Catania *autostrada*. Hotel comfortable and best bet for meals.

Pisa, 56100 Tuscany

Roma   Double with bath *$36*
Via Bonanno 111   Telephone (050)22698

The leaning tower, cathedral and most of Pisa's other sights are just outside your balcony window. No restaurant here.

Pompei, 80045 Compania

Delle Rose   Double with bath *$26*
Via Bartolo Longo   Telephone (081)8631854

Pompei is usually a day-trip for most, but we found the evenings enjoyable and this very modest place just fine. Good location.

Positano, 84017 Campania

Palazzo Murat   Double with bath *$42*
Center of village   Telephone (089)875117

A sumptuous baroque villa of antique-filled rooms, balconies, and patio breakfasts beneath a waterfall of flaming bougainvillea and hibiscus.

Rapallo, 16035 Liguria

De La Promenade   Double with bath *$30*
Piazza Garibaldi   Telephone (0185)50021

Beat bayfront prices at this 20-year favorite in town center. Nearby *Elite* restaurant is a delight for Ligurian seafood.

Ravenna, 48100 Emilia-Romagna

Capello
Via IV Novembre 41

Double with bath *$30*
Telephone (0544)22306

Fine old converted villa on quiet, walking street near market and Piazza del Popolo, as gay and Venetian as Piazza San Marco.

Ravello, 84010 Campania

Parsifal ex Convento

Double with bath *$32*
Telephone (089)857144

Augustinian monks founded this former convent-cloister in 12th century high above Almalfi coast. You won't forget it.

Rimini, 47037 Emilia-Romagna

Metropole
Viale Regina Elena 64

Double with bath *$26*
Telephone (0541)81059

Modern and but a few steps from Rimini's beautiful beach where you'll have your own cabana. Adriatic coast crowded in season.

Rome, 00100 Lazio

Sole al Pantheon
Piazza della Rotunda 63
00186 Rome

Double with bath *$48*
Telephone (06)6793490

Long our favorite hotel and neighborhood in Rome. A 16th-century villa on glorious piazza and a short walk from Piazza Navona, the city's living room. Area a warren of great little restaurants.

Delle Muse
Via Tommaso Salvini 18
00197 Rome

Double with bath *$42*
Telephone (06)870095

A family owned hotel-pension in swank Parioli area just outside central city. Outdoor dining in garden and helpful staff.

Raphael
Largo Febo 2
00186 Rome

Double with bath *$66*
Telephone (06)6569051

Another old favorite off Piazza Navona with every convenience yet a most elegant air of Renaissance Italy. Fine rooftop terrace.

Scalinata di Spagna
Piazza Trinita dei Monte 17
00187 Rome

Double with bath *$40*
Telephone (06)6793006

Neat, cheerful but modest pension with great location at top of Spanish Steps. Catch is mid-city noise and 10-room capacity.

D'Inghilterra
Via Bocca di Leone 14
00187 Rome

Double with bath *$76*
Telephone (06)672161

For those who want Rome's finest small hotel in perfect location near Spanish Steps, Via Condotti shopping, fine restaurants.

San Gimignano, 53037 Tuscany

La Cisterna
Piazza Cisterna

Double with bath *$42*
Telephone (0577)940328

Exquisite 15th-century inn at center of Tuscan hill town noted for its towers. Its *La Terrazze* restaurant one of region's best.

Scanno, 67038 Abruzzo

Centrale
Center of village

Double with bath *$30*
Telephone (0864)91332

One of region's charming and typical towns where women wear Abruzzo costumes all week! Hearty local food in dining room.

Siena, 53100 Tuscany

La Toscana
Via C. Angiolieri 12

Double with bath *$42*
Telephone (0577)46097

A former palace built in 1228 by a Florentine family and a bit difficult to reach by car on narrow streets. Worth the effort.

| Gardin | Double with bath *$45* |
| Via Custoza 2 | Telephone (0577)47056 |

This 16th-century country house on outskirts has swimming pool, garden dining, a nice bar and it's a longtime favorite with us.

Syracuse, 96100 Sicily

| AGIP Motel | Double with bath *$41* |
| Viale Teracati 30 | Telephone (0931)66944 |

Absolute best location for visiting town's Greek and Roman ruins. Air conditioned and taxi/bus ride into old city on port a short one.

Sirmione, 25019 Lombardy

| Du Lac | Double with bath *$42* |
| Via 25 Aprile 46 | Telephone (030)916026 |

Your own private beach in sunny "island" town jutting from south shore of Lake Garda. Summer crowds fill hotel

---

Taormina, 98039 Sicily

| Villa Paradiso | Double with bath *$45* |
| Via Roma 6 | Telephone (0942)23922 |

Antiques in every corner, radiant Turkish rugs strewn about and a fourth-floor dining room known across Sicily for food and view.

| Villa Nettuno | Double with bath *$36* |
| Via L. Pirandello 33 | Telephone (0942)23797 |

A miniature Moorish castle of Pompei red, dining terrace alive with flowers and owner Maria Sciglio as friendly as sunshine.

Urbino, 61029 Marche

| Italia | Double with bath *$36* |
| Corso Garibaldi 32 | Telephone (0722)2701 |

Most convenient location for visiting everything in this often overlooked but glorious town. Superior regional food also.

Venice, 30100 Veneto

Patria-Tre Rose
Calle dei Fabbri 905 30124   X

Double with bath *$50*
Telephone (041)22940

Our Venetian favorite since the 50s and just a step behind St. Marks Square. No restaurant but others on busy little street.

Locanda Cipriani
Island of Torcello 30012

Double with bath *$65*
Telephone (041)730150

Surely the most elegant "rustic" inn on earth. Remote, but wondrous dining and exquisite setting will live in your memory forever.

Accademia
Dorsoduro/
Ponte Maravegie 30123

Double with bath *$42*
Telephone (041)710188

An old villa that seems a microcosm of the city itself. Compact garden, dining room and bar, family feeling. Quiet beyond belief.

San Fantin
Campiello La Fenice 30124

Double with bath *$45*
Telephone (041)31401

A tiny one with exterior more impressive than within, but price is right and it's near restaurants to fit any pocketbook.

Atlantide
Calle Misericordia 375-a 30121

Double with bath *$40*
Telephone (041)716901

Very modest but near railway station and budget dining on Lista di Spagna. Friendly owners have another small hotel nearby.

Bisanzio
Calle della Pieta 3651 2122

Double with bath *$54*
Telephone (041)703100

Another late-Renaissance inn just outside the center and toward the old arsenal. Most comfortable and the crowds thin here.

Verona, 37100 Veneto

Colomba d'Oro
Via Cattaneo 10

Double with bath *$54*
Telephone (045)595300

A few steps from Verona's breathtaking Piazza Bra, the Roman arena and a galaxy of good restaurants. Our favorite since 50s when Verona was our hometown for almost three years.

Arena
Porta Palio 2

Double with bath *$38*
Telephone (045)32440

Another good location for seeing one of Italy's most enchanting cities. Small and easy on your budget. You'll dine more than well at *Pedavena,* Piazza Bra, and *Torcoloti,* Via Zambelli 24.

Vicenza, 36100 Veneto

Cristina
Corso San Felice 32

Double with bath *$40*
Telephone (0444)34280

Our visits to Palladio's town are always made pleasant by a stay in this neat little place. *Tre Visi* best for local dining.

Basilica
Piazza delle Erbe 9

Double with bath *$34*
Telephone (0444)21204

In the market at the heart of everything, right beside Palladio's stunning basilica. Small, modest and food fresh from market.

One of the best values for motorists in Italy is a string of motels run by *AGIP,* the giant Italian petroleum company. They are usually located just off an *autostrada* or on the outskirts of a town, with rates in the $35-45 range for a very neat and efficient double room with private bath. Many have dining rooms. They're all over the peninsula, so keep an eye out for the bold yellow *AGIP* sign with its many-footed dragon.

St. Hubert / Clervaux

Luxembourg

The Grand Duchy of Luxembourg is hardly larger than its name, measuring less than 1,000 square miles in area and no more than 60 by 40 miles at its longest and widest points. Within this small country live 360 thousand hearty souls, each of whom seems to have his arms extended in welcome to visitors. No matter that the languages spoken here are *Letzeburgesch*, German, French and more than a sprinkling of English. Or that the food is basically French with inroads of German cooking. Or that the Belgian *franc* as well as the

Luxembourg *franc* are both legal tender. Luxembourgers are content to sit in their lovely little enclave, sip Moselle wines or glorious Luxembourg beer with their formidable meals and let other Europeans occupy themselves in economic and political tug-of-wars.

The little country really has a bit of everything: a capital city that was once the greatest fortress in Europe and still looks the part; a northeast region that shares Germany's Eifel mountains to create a little Switzerland; the incomparable forests of the Ardennes to the west; and the Moselle River valley carving its southeastern border with Germany. In between is enough fertile farmland and well-camouflaged industry to give Luxembourg one of Europe's highest living standards, plus near-zero unemployment.

Icelandic Airlines will fly you to Luxembourg from the US and their fares are as good as you will find for regularly scheduled lines. *Air Canada* will get you to Paris for a change to *Luxair. Hertz, Avis, InterRent, Europcar* and *Colux* will rent you a *Fiat 127, Opel Kadett* or similar for about $200 a week unlimited mileage, plus 10% tax. Fuel is now around $2 per gallon.

Luxembourg National Railways runs the country's trains and buses, accepts *Eurailpass* and has 1, 5 and 10-day network tickets also good on buses. These tickets offer substantial savings on first-class fares, normally about .06 per kilometer, and there is a 50% reduction for all over 65 years old. With distances so short, there is no way to spend much traveling within Luxembourg.

The Luxembourg *franc* is currency, divided into 100 *centimes* and pegged to the neighboring Belgian *franc* in value, currently about .02 or 50 to the US dollar. Banking hours 9:00-12:00 and 2:00-4:00, five days, with stores open 8:00-12:00 and 2:00-6:00 p.m., six days, except for Mondays when they are closed in the morning. Voltage is 220. Luxembourg has fairly typical European weather, which means 60s in summer and 30s in winter, the latter always depending on altitude.

You won't find a great deal of space devoted to Luxembourg's dishes in the world's cookbooks and the reason is simple. Nothing really stands out for the way it is prepared. The country abounds in game, but it is usually cooked with but slight variations on Belgian-French or German recipes. Trout, crayfish, pike and other fresh water fish are normally just grilled or deep fried with a minimum of fanfare, and of course landlocked Luxembourg does not have a fleet of trawlers hauling seafood from the Atlantic and Mediterranean to its tables.

But smoked Ardennes ham is a plentiful delicacy here, as it is in Belgium, and the young white wines from Moselle slopes give a festive air to any meal. You will see your share and more of potatoes, dumplings and other Teutonic staples, which is fine when they accompany a game ragout as they often do.

Luxembourg city is moderate to expensive, the smaller towns much less costly.

Hotels & Inns

Clervaux

St. Hubert   Double with bath *$32*
Clervaux-Reuler 3   Telephone (352)91023

Clervaux lies in northern Luxembourg's section of the magnificent Ardennes Forest, a medieval jewel set in countryside that has every lure for an extended holiday. A half-mile from town center you will find the chalet *St. Hubert* a perfect place to spend a few days.

Claravallis   Double with bath *$38*
3 rue de la Gare   Telephone (352)91034

In town and convenient to the railway station, *Claravallis* is a modern version of the local chalet architecture with every amenity, most rooms with private balconies. All meals served.

Echternach

Etoile d'Or
39 rue de la Gare

Double with bath *$22*
Telephone (352)72095

Another remarkable medieval town on the German border, this one at the heart of Luxembourg's "Little Switzerland," where you will find *Etoile d'Or* both comfortable and easy on your budget.

Esch-sur-Sure

Du Moulin
6 rue du Moulin

Double with bath *$22*
Telephone (352)89107

Du Moulin has the perfect location in this tiny Ardennes market town practically surrounded by Sure River and watched over by an ancient castle. All 27 rooms with baths and it's another budget haven for your Luxembourg visit.

Gaichel

La Bonne Auberge
Village center

Double with bath *$33*
Telephone (352)39140

Gaichel lies on Belgian border in midst of even more spectacular scenery. Hotel known for some of the best food in Luxembourg, especially its preparation of wild game from lush surrounding countryside.

Grevenmacher

De la Poste
28 rue de Treves

Double with bath *$25*
Telephone (352)75136

Prepare yourself for the finest of Moselle wines as Grevenmacher is the district capital, right on the German border. *Poste* has only 12 rooms, so book ahead for visit.

Luxembourg City

Alfa
16 Place de la Gare

Double with bath *$42*
Telephone (352)490011

A longtime fixture on the local scene and brace yourself for a facade that looks like the town fortress, but all 100 rooms are spacious and it's convenient to railway station. All meals served.

| Beaumont | Double with bath *$26* |
| 11 rue Beaumont | Telephone (352)25237 |

Only 12 rooms here, but it does have certain other virtues, like good location in old city and all rooms with baths. An excellent choice in the moderate price range.

| Cheminee de Paris | Double with bath *$44* |
| 10 rue d'Anvers | Telephone (352)492931 |

A relatively new hotel in the southern section of city with 23 rooms and restaurant serving hearty Luxembourg fare. Also near main station.

Mondorf-les-Bains

| Windsor | Double with bath *$27* |
| 19 Ave. des Bains | Telephone (352)67203 |

A small, tidy inn in pretty Gander River spa town on the country's southeast border with France. Just 17 rooms, but all meals served and kitchen favorably influenced by nearness to France.

Vianden

| Heintz | Double with bath *$38* |
| 55 Grand'rue | Telephone (352)84155 |

An old Trinitarian monastery, family run for three generations, that also houses the outstanding *Hostellerie des Trinitaires* restaurant. Hotel a good value, but dining can be very expensive here.

| Victor Hugo | Double with bath *$27* |
| 1 rue Victor Hugo | Telephone (352)84160 |

Victor Hugo a bit more moderate in cost and another good reason to visit this charming town on the northeast border with Germany. River Our, Ardennes/Eifel Mountains scenery and majestic castle make 9th-century village one of Luxembourg's most beautiful and popular destinations. We can't wait to return.

Ambassade / Amsterdam

Netherlands

Some countries disappoint visitors by not living up to the collection of visual images they have formed before arrival, aided by tourist office posters and travel brochures. Not so the Netherlands. Here is the land of Hans Brinker, tulip fields, dikes and canals lacing the landscape, cheese, bicycles, windmills and wooden shoes, Rembrandt paintings, pea soup, *polders* and jovial citizens anxious to share their good life with any and all. It is also small enough so that you really needn't miss too much, given a reasonable amount of time and an adventurous spirit.

About 40 percent of the country is below sea level, the man-made *polders* being protected by dikes and drained by canals. All this irrigation leads to fertile land indeed, and Dutch larders reflect it in their abundance. The lakes of Friesland to the north are a frequently overlooked and very rewarding area, as are the islands and peninsulas of Zeeland near the southwest border with Belgium.

The Dutch have a word, *gezellig*, which describes their country, its capital, Amsterdam, and even their lifestyle. It means cozy, warm, not too large, colorful and filled with all sorts of small and satisfying delights. That's Holland in a nutshell.

KLM, Finnair and *Transamerica* will fly you to Amsterdam from the US; *Canadian Pacific* and *KLM* from Canada. *Hertz, Avis, Van Wijk, Budget, Kaspers & Lotte* and *Godfrey Davis* will rent you a *Fiat 127* or similar for about $170 per week unlimited mileage, plus 18% tax. Fuel for it will cost $2.50 per gallon at this writing.

Netherlands Railways honor your *Eurailpass* and have a 7-day pass of their own costing approximately $60 first-class, $40 second, and it's good for a 50% reduction on inter-urban bus lines. From May through September Dutch railways offer one-day round-trips to the more attractive towns and areas of Holland, including whatever bus or boat transportation is required. Pick up brochures for these trips as well as tickets from railway offices. Bus service is a shade more expensive than rail travel, but most cities have very inexpensive day-tickets, tours and excursion rates to other cities. Dutch *VVV* tourist information offices throughout the country have a wealth of information on bus and rail travel, plus other helpful services.

Dutch currency is the *guilder* or *florin* as it is sometimes called. It is now worth .36 cents US or 2.78 to the dollar. Banks are open five days from 9:00-4:00, stores generally 9:00 to 5:30-6:00, Saturdays until 4:00. Voltage is 220. Average temperatures in summer are in the 60s, winters usually in the high 30s.

Holland's food has the same character as its people: sturdy, comforting and easy-to-know. Green pea soup laced with sausage and pork strips comes near being the national dish and it's delicious. Look for *erwtensoep* on your menu. Herring is another national craze and you will find street stands everywhere offering it *al fresco* layered with chopped raw onion. *Hutspot met klapstuk* is a meat-and-vegetable stew that reflects ingredients from the region in which it is served, all of them robust. The Dutch love mussels almost as much as the Belgians and you will find them everywhere in season. Huge Zeeland oysters are a delicacy and 26 varieties of home-grown cheeses will spread a lot of crackers.

Two dining experiences shouldn't be missed in Holland. The first is a visit to a *broodjeswinkel,* or delicatessen-sandwich shop, for a selection of cold and warm open-faced sandwiches. The other is a *rijsttafel* (rice table) luncheon or dinner of from six to 26 highly spiced Indonesian dishes; meat, vegetables, seafood, chicken and fruits, all eaten with rice and a hot sauce that would jolt any Mexican. More than 700 Dutch restaurants participate in the *Tourist Menu* plan, an excellent three-course meal for about $7.50, and *VVV* offices will give you a list of their addresses.

For the past few years the Dutch have been doing everything they can to hold down prices for their visitors, with admirable success. Amsterdam can still be an expensive city, unless you watch your budget, but smaller towns and villages offer a measure of relief.

Hotels & Inns
(Bed and Breakfast)

Amsterdam, Noord Holland

De la Poste   Double with bath *$35*
5 Reguliersgracht   Telephone (020)237105

Amsterdam's narrow "canal houses" date from the city's 17th-century Golden Age and the *Poste* remains one of the best values of the lot. Finest location in town, *gezellig* atmosphere, precipitous stairwells, small and usually modest rooms. We've been coming back for two decades, never expecting luxury.

Ambassade   Double with bath *$45-56*
34 Herengracht   Telephone (020)262333

Several canal houses joined together to form one of the city's most enchanting hotels. Exquisite antique furnishings in public rooms, most bedrooms facing the canal and the finest of Dutch breakfasts of eggs, cheese, meat and a galaxy of breads. Most visitors love it and so do we.

Die Port van Cleve   Double with bath *$56-82*
178 N.Z. Voorburgwal   Telephone (020)244860

Don't despair, these prices could put you in a four-poster bed and other trappings of a 17th-century Dutch burgher successful in the tulip trade. Restaurant famous throughout world for its glorious steaks and charm of the Delft-blue tile frieze of children ringing the walls. Whatever your hotel, please dine here once.

Canal House   Double with bath *$36-46*
148 Keizersgracht   Telephone (020)225182

All the amenities and charm of the *Ambassade,* which

extend to bedrooms with 18-foot ceilings, period furniture, enormous baths and a general feeling of sleeping in a Mozart drawing room. Regal bar, lovely garden and everyone is captivated on sight.

Arnhem, Gelderland

Postiljon Motel
25 Europaweg
off E36

Double with bath *$25-35*
Telephone (085)453741

Most convenient for motorists who would like to see the nearby Open Air Museum of 60 typical homes, farm houses, cottages and windmills from the 17th to 19th centuries. A charming display.

Bergen, Noord Holland

Zee-Bergen
11 Wilhelminalaan

Double with bath *$34-46*
Telephone (02208)2472

This small 20-room place on outskirts of town is noted for its fine Dutch food. Three miles from North Sea beaches and a short drive to cheese market town of Alkmaar.

Bolsward, Friesland

De Wijnberg
5 Marktplein

Double with bath *$32-36*
Telephone (05157)2220

A little charmer right on busy Market Square that captures the feeling of this ancient town perfectly. Dining room noted for its Frisian regional food, or just have a cool Dutch beer at table on square and enjoy the activity.

Breda, Noord Brabant

Huis Den Deijl
8 Marellenweg
S of city center

Double (no private baths) *$28-32*
Telephone (076)653616

A tiny and very picturesque cottage hidden in Mastbos Forest. Typical country furnishings and exceptional Dutch food. Only eight rooms and this is a stop worth calling ahead for.

Delft, Zuid Holland

Juliana
33 Maerten Trompstraat

Double with bath *$36-40*
Telephone (015)567612

Readers have for years joined us in praising this fine little hotel in one of the country's most enchanting towns. You'll like everything about the *Juliana:* garden, terrace, dining and a most friendly welcome. We look forward to a return.

Eindhoven, Noord Brabant

Park
18 Alberdinck Thijmlaan

Double with bath *$35*
Telephone (040)114100

Set in a lovely park on the south edge of city center, it has a good restaurant, pleasant terrace, most comforts and, best of all, gets you out of bustling Eindhoven.

Epe, Gelderland

Hof van Gelre
46 Hoofdstraat

Double with bath *$38*
Telephone (05780)12232

Epe is set on the edge of the country's largest forest and this small hotel reaps the benefits with excellent local game served hot from its kitchen. Only 11 rooms and area a tourist haven, so plan ahead on this one.

Goes, Zeeland

Terminus
37 Frans den Hollanderlaan

Double with bath *$28*
Telephone (01100)27501

Eurailpass holders frequently seek an excellent hotel near train station and this one faces it. Old but recently remodeled, its kitchen is noted for treatment of Zeeland's marvelous fish.

Graveland, Noord Holland

Wapen van Amsterdam
129 Noordereinde

Double with bath *$33-43*
Telephone (035)61661

Many hotels gain their reputations for superior food and *Wapen* is one of them. Only 12 rooms in this old coaching stop and the rustic dining room and flower-decked terrace add to its charm.

The Hague, Zuid Holland

Corona   Double with bath *$50-56*
Buitenhof 41   Telephone (070)637930

A sprightly and colorful small hotel at city center with an always active sidewalk cafe beneath its orange awnings. Faces Buitenhof Square and very convenient to everything in town. Only 23 rooms.

Maastricht, Limburg

Beaumont   Double with bath *$36-42*
Stationstraat   Telephone (043)54433

Maastricht, our favorite town in Holland, is a glorious little city that lives up to its "Burgundian" boast in food and life-style. *Beaumont* a rather plain looking hotel, but rooms are comfortable and dining room holds its head high in food-loving Maastricht.

Stijns   Double with bath *$35*
Stationstraat   Telephone (043)51651

A small, family style hotel convenient to station with only 17 rooms. Yet it maintains a restaurant and we find it comfortable enough for budget-conscious travelers.

Noordwijk, Zuid Holland

Marie Rose   Double with bath *$35-42*
25 Emmaweg   Telephone (01719)12697

Hardly a year goes by that we don't receive letters from readers praising the *Marie Roses's* friendly owners and all-round comfort. Most of them also mention the *goede keuken* served here.

Rotterdam, Zuid Holland

Pax   Double with bath *$42*
658 Schiekade   Telephone (010)653107

If you want a moderate mid-city hotel in Rotterdam, this is

it. Near main railway station, air terminal and not too far from Boymans van Beuningen Museum with a magnificent collection of Old Masters and modern art. Don't miss it.

Scheveningen, Zuid Holland (The Hague)

Bali
1 Badhuisweg

Double with bath *$34*
Telephone (070)503500

One of Holland's best Indonesian restaurants in country's foremost beach resort, the *Bali* also has 34 rooms in a wondrous old building a few blocks from North Sea. Few Dutch realize water is too cold for swimming!

Van der Spek
18 Antwerpsestraat

Double with bath *$36*
Telephone (070)556831

Scheveningen is a lovely old fashioned resort and *Van der Spek* fits into the local scene perfectly with its turn-of-century architecture. Restaurant, 14 rooms and lots of Dutch warmth.

Valkenburg, Limburg

Prinses Juliana
11 Broekhem

Double with bath *$40-73*
Telephone (04406)12244

After sampling the considerable delights of Maastricht seven miles to the west, treat yourself to more of Holland's best regional food in the region's best dining room, *Juliana*. We can think of no better place to spend a few days in Holland. Beautiful town, marvelous hotel, food to make the gods rejoice.

Utne / Utne

Norway

Here is a country that takes two of nature's most inspiring sights, majestic mountains and rugged shoreline, and entwines them into a 12,000-mile coastline that is almost overpowering in its beauty. Norway's western coast is an endless filigree of *fjords* and offshore islands, etching and carving the shore in a way you will find no place else on earth. Nor do you have to travel 1,300 miles to Norway's North Cape beyond the Arctic Circle to experience this stunning scenery: you will find lovely and dramatic *fjords* within an hour's drive of Oslo.

Norwegians are a hardy lot, almost as much so as their Viking forebears, with very little arable land at their command for sustenance. What little farmland there is can be found hanging precariously from a slope above a mist-shrouded *fjord* or lake, making them as adept as the Swiss at digging potatoes from a hillside. Yet their fishing fleet is huge as well as colorful and they net more fish than any other country in Europe.

Birch trees carpet the countryside, the midnight sun hangs through the summer months beyond the Arctic Circle, northern lights flash through winter nights and the people, from Oslo to Narvik, are among Europe's friendliest. We can hardly wait to return.

SAS and *Icelandic* will fly you there from the US; *Air Canada* and *SAS* from Canada. *SAS* and *Braathens SAFE*, the Norwegian domestic airline, will zip you to the far reaches of this elongated country in their swift jets. *Scandinavia Car Rental*, *Hertz* and *Avis* will charge about $290 per week for a Ford *Fiesta*, unlimited mileage, plus 20% tax. And expect fuel for it to cost around $2.50 per gallon.

Your *Eurailpass* is good on *NSB*, the Norwegian State Railways, and they also participate in the *Nordturist Med Tag* ticket with Sweden, Denmark and Finland. That's 21 days of train travel in Scandinavia for $151 second-class, $227 first-class and children under 12 for half that. A full month will cost you $189 second-class, $285 first. Bus service is very important in Norway, particularly if you care to visit small fishing villages along the rugged west coast or explore north of the Arctic Circle.

Norway's currency is the *krone* and it's divided into 100 *ore*, the *krone* being now worth .14 US or 7.14 to the dollar. Banks are usually open from 10:00-3:00, five days, stores from 9:00-5:00 or 6:00, noon on Saturdays and Thursday evenings. Voltage is 220.

Temperatures obviously vary considerably in a country that stretches 1,500 miles north-south, but count on 50s and 60s in summer, almost always below freezing between November and March.

Rustic, straightforward and strong are words that come to mind in describing Norwegian cooking. How else to characterize venison or reindeer roasted with goat cheese sauce, salt-cured mutton chops, horseradish butter, fish salad with horseradish sauce, herring for breakfast and that most puzzling of all Norwegian dishes, *lutefisk*. The latter is cod, dried for months outside, then soaked for days in a birch-ashes lye solution, boiled with salt and eaten after a liberal splash of melted pork fat. You may be a bit offended by its texture, but not by its taste: the non-Norwegian consensus is that there isn't any.

Picture an American Thanksgiving table and you have a fair idea of the typical Norwegian breakfast, an endless array of meats, fish, cheeses and bread. One of the cheeses might well be *gammelost*, a molded cheese made from sour rather than fresh milk. An elderly Norwegian innkeeper friend in California always insisted on his *gammelost* for breakfast, frequently offering to share with unsuspecting guests. In 25 years we never saw anyone get beyond the first tentative and jolting nibble.

Norway's prices fall somewhere between those of Finland and Sweden-Denmark, which makes it middle ground for Scandinavia. Oslo is expensive, with towns and villages in the countryside falling to medium-priced.

Hotels & Inns

Bergen, 5000 Hordaland

Strand | Double with bath *$55*
Strandkaien 2 | Telephone (05)310815

Right on the busy waterfront, 55 rooms, breakfast only and if cost strikes you as steep for a B&B, then prepare yourself for Norwegian prices. But the picturesque harbor and old wooden houses of Bergen really shouldn't be missed.

Brevik, 3950 Telemark

Korvetten | Double with bath *$55-59*
On highway E18 | Telephone (035)71166

A modern motor hotel in this colorful *fjord* town 94 miles south of Oslo. All meals served, fantastic sightseeing in area and children under 12 stay free here.

Bykle, 4694 Aust Agder

Bykle Hotell

Double (no private baths) *$42*
Telephone (043/38)100-10

Norway's most picturesque valley awaits the visitor to Bykle with its 13th-century church and silversmith shops. Lots of good fishing in river. Difficult to reach but worth it.

Egersund, 4370 Rogaland

Eiger Motel
Edge of town

Double with bath *$45*
Telephone (044)90200

A modern place with 20 rooms on the coastal road south of Stavanger. Lots of sailing and water sports in Egersund's protected harbor. Good restaurant with, of course, plenty of fresh seafood.

Elveseter, 2687 Oppland (Boverdalen)

Elveseter Turisthotell
2689 Elveseter

Double with bath *$28-36*
Telephone (062)12000

Really out of the way in the Jotunheimen Mountains northwest of Lillehammer, but the scenery is magnificent and readers are in love with the hotel, an old farmhouse that just grew and grew.

Geilo, 3580 Buskerud

Alpin

Double with bath *$55*
Telephone (067)85544

A good midway stop on Oslo-Bergen road and also one of Norway's most popular winter/summer resort areas. Hotel open year-round, but full pension service in winter season only. *Alpin* looks like its name, a typical Norwegian mountain house.

Geilo Hotel
Postboks 113

Double with bath *$61*
Telephone (067)85511

An old coaching stop, built in 1876, that still maintains a feeling for the past. Family run, the *Geilo's* colorful country-antique furnishings and excellent food will make your stay a pleasant one.

Gol, 3550 Buskerud

Eidsgaard

Double with bath *$47-57*
Telephone (067)74955

Another good stopover point on Oslo-Bergen road, this one a Norwegian-style chalet with open fireplaces, bar and full dining service, including pension for an extended stay.

Grotli, 2695 Oppland

Grotli Hoyfjells
On E 15

Double with bath *$48-55*
Telephone (062)13912

More fabulous scenery and another hotel that fits in perfectly, a complex of Norwegian-style farmhouses with every comfort and a dining room offering lots of local food, including plenty of fish and game. Join Scandinavian guests in the hotel's sauna.

Lillehammer, 2600 Oppland

Rustad Fjellstue
Sjusjoen 2612

Double with bath *$34-38*
Telephone (065)63408

A wondrous lakeside mountain resort 12 miles northeast of Lillehammer. Another place where you may have your daily sauna, followed by a dip in the freezing lake!

Lom, 2686 Oppland

Fossheim
On E 15

Double with bath *$39*
Telephone (062)11005

Typical Norwegian hotel on the scenic Grotli-Geiranger road, this one with rooms in the main building or in charming little cottages just made for a family stopover. Lots of stave churches in Oppland.

Norheimsund, 5600 Hordaland

Bergly Pensionat

Double with bath *$34-38*
Telephone (055)51059

Only ten rooms in this modest place right on Hardangerfjord about 50 miles east of Bergen. Breakfast included and dinner here is about $5 per person. Pure Norwegian food and a bargain.

Oslo, 1000

Stefan
Rosenkrantzgate 1
Oslo 1

Double with bath *$58-68*
Telephone (02)336290

A warm and inviting hotel right in the middle of downtown Oslo that is noted with locals for its spectacular "cold table" at lunchtime. Manager Erling Overby pitches in to make each guest's stay a pleasant one and watches the dining room with a hawk's eye.

Forbunds
Holbergsplass 1
Oslo 1

Double with bath *$59-63*
Telephone (02)208855

Mid-city location a step from *Hotel Scandinavia,* a highrise Oslo landmark where SAS airline buses stop. *Forbunds* resembles a stately opera house, but the interior is modern and comfortable with notable dining room as well. Rooms without private baths much less expensive here and at *Stefan* above.

Vettakollen
Huldreveien 14
Oslo 3

Double (no private baths) *$44*
Telephone (02)145590

An older hotel high above Oslo outskirts in peaceful wooded terrain. Bracing air and good for budget. Full dining room and children under 12 stay free.

Gabelshus
Gabelsgate 16
Oslo 2

Double with bath *$64-70*
Telephone (02)562590

A marvelous hotel in the pleasant west-end residential section of Oslo. Lots of antiques and a bit on the formal side, but fine dining and beautiful garden. A very English feeling here.

IMI Hotel
Staffeldtsgate 4
Oslo 1

Double with bath *$58*
Telephone (02)205330

A modern and efficient hotel in the central district. All 60 rooms with baths and the dining room has a special daily menu.

Stavanger, 4000 Rogaland

Rogalandsheimen
Near train station

Double (no private baths) *$32*
Telephone (04)520188

Small, very modest and breakfast only served here, but it's convenient for rail travelers and the price is soothing.

Trondheim, 7000 Sor Trondelag

IMI Hotel
Kongensgate 26

Double with bath *$62*
Telephone (075)28348

A sister "mission hotel" to the Oslo *IMI,* which means comfort and efficiency, plus straightforward Norwegian food at fairly moderate prices in the dining room.

Ulvik, 5730 Hordaland

Brakanes
On Hardangerfjord

Double with bath *$37-45*
Telephone (055)26105

Majesty is the only word for fjord scenery and the *Brakanes* has one of the best views of all. It also has every amenity and regular guests year after year, a marvelous spot to break your trip for a few days. Water sports are a way of life here.

Utne, 5797 Hordaland

Hotel Utne
Village center

Double with bath *$48*
Telephone (054)66983

Utne's spectacular setting at the tip of a promontory between Hardangerfjord and Sorfjord (due east of Bergen) makes it easier to reach by ferry from Kinsarvik or Kvanndal. They stop right in front of the hotel and there are several daily. Both the village and hotel offer everything you could want for a Norwegian countryside holiday: fjord scenery, a colorful and typical inn, lots of good food, miles and miles of virgin land for walking.

Voss, 5700 Hardaland

Bavallstova   Double with bath *$28-32*
1000 feet above town   Telephone (055)11873

The Oslo-Bergen railway will take you to Voss above Hardangerfjord. This mountainside retreat has 15 double rooms, all with baths, and offers half-pension to its guests, a good idea considering the remote site.

Fleischer's Motel   Double with bath *$49-54*
On lake   Telephone (055)11155

These cabins of from two to six beds serve as an annex to the traditional, older and more expensive *Hotel Fleischer,* a lovely Voss fixture for years. Cabins have kitchens, refrigerators and private baths, but you may still take full or half-pension.

Pousada da Sao Bras / Sao Bras de Alportal

Portugal

Few countries in all of Europe offer a visitor such value as Portugal, a situation brought about by several factors. First, the Portuguese *escudo* is currently worth about one US cent, a drop of 60 percent in value during the past decade. Secondly, and more difficult to understand, is that Portugal has never had the number of visitors that other western European countries look forward to each summer. Yet the scenery is just as dramatic as that of some of its neighbors, the cuisine just as "exotic," the wines superb and hotels and restaurants are quickly rising to Continental standards. Two dozen government-owned *pousadas* blanket the country, providing excellent accommodations in converted palaces, castles, monasteries and other historic buildings while serving colorful regional dishes in their dining rooms. Even car rental is much less expensive in Portugal.

Lisbon is a capital city in the true sense, with grand boulevards, spacious parks and plazas, the enchanting old Alfama district with its narrow, twisting streets, a lively waterfront along the Tagus River and the rainbow of pastel-colored buildings that give a unique character to the town. The sunny Algarve beneath the chin of Portugal's Atlantic coast is fast becoming one of Europe's more desirable, and inexpensive, watering holes. Nazare on the western coast, while a bit more commercial today, still has its fishermen in colorful dress dragging their gaily painted boats onto the beach several times a day. The old university city of Coimbra is a delight and the old walled city of Evora southeast of Lisbon is an enchanting mix of Moorish-Roman-Renaissance architecture, everyone's favorite.

The Portuguese airline *TAP* and *TWA* will fly you from the US; *Air Canada* and *TAP* from Canada. *Hertz, Avis, Contauto, Flamingo* and *InterRent* will provide a *Fiat 127* or *Morris Mini* for $179 a week unlimited mileage, plus 7% tax. Fuel for it will cost you about $2.85 per gallon at this writing.

Portuguese Railways accepts your *Eurailpass* and has its own Tourist Ticket good for 7, 14 or 21 days at a cost of $42, 67 and 96. Bus service is generally good throughout the country and the system is tied to the *Europabus* network.

The *escudo* is Portuguese currency, made up of 100 *centavos,* and it is now worth .011 or 91 per dollar. Banking hours are 9:00-12:00 and 2:00-3:30, five days. Stores are generally open from 9:00-1:00 and again from 3:00-7:00, with most of them closed on Saturday afternoons. Voltage is again 220. Portugal's climate is ideal, with summers almost always in the 70s and winters seldom lower than the 50s.

Portuguese menus are never lacking in seafood, particularly the ever-present *bacalhau* or salt cod, which is quite good in a variety of casseroles or braised with herbs in small cakes. Swordfish is usually available and always excellent if broiled or grilled simply. *Caldeirada*, a fish and shellfish stew, is a fixture along the coast but it may also contain freshwater fish as well. *Caldo verde*, a fresh kale, potato and ham or sausage soup, rivals *bacalhau* as the national dish, and lamb, pork and veal are all plentiful and very good. *Cozido* is the Portuguese version of Spain's boiled meat dish and just as tasty.

Portuguese wines making their way to the Western Hemisphere are usually the ports and roses, but there are fine table wines in many parts of the country. *Vinhos verdes,* white or red, are most refreshing and have a slight effervescence that falls short of making them bubbly. You'll enjoy them with almost anything.

Portugal, as we said at the outset, is balm to your budget, the sort of place we all look for but seldom find these days. Count your *escudos* while you count your blessings!

Hotels & Inns

Braganca, 5300 Montanhas

Pousada de Sao Bartolomeu   Double with bath *$32.50*
Estrada de Turismo   Telephone 22493

Near the old walled town of Braganca beside the Tras-os-Montes mountains, this contemporary inn near the northern border with Spain offers its guests relief from the remote countryside. Local ham, sausages and regional wine are menu fixtures here. Most comfortable, and reasonable rates include breakfasts.

Canicada, 4850 Costa Verde

Pousada de Sao Bento   Double with bath *$44.50*
30 miles NE of Braga   Telephone 57190

This rough stone inn high above a lovely river in the northern province of Minho is everything a weary traveler looks forward to at sunset. Excellent food and drink, pleasant rooms and its own pool for humid summer evenings.

Caramulo, 3475 Montanhas

Pousada de Sao Jeronimo	Double with bath *$32.50*
24 miles W of Viseu	Telephone 86291

One mile east of the village you will find this modern inn with six rooms, inland from the main coastal road and about 45 miles north of Coimbra. The setting is remote, but the countryside lovely. Again, there is a pool for that cooling dip before dinner.

Cascais, 2750 Lisbon Coast

Estalagem do Farol	Double with bath *$44*
Estrada da Boca do Inferno 7	Telephone 280173

An older place with 20 rooms and a marvelous location, on the southern tip of town near the lighthouse. It also has a pool, tennis court and luscious seafood ever present in the dining room.

Hotel do Guincho	Double with bath *$64*
NW of town on beach	Telephone 2850491

A truly exceptional hotel built on the site of a 17th-century fortress, a rock promontory jutting into the Atlantic five minutes west of Cascais. Bedrooms floored with old tile, public rooms a regal delight and a dining room that served us the finest sea bass we've ever had. You'll never forget this one.

Castelo do Bode, 2300 Planicies

Pousada de Sao Pedro	Double with bath *$32.50*
10 miles S of Tomar	Telephone 38159

A stately white manor house set in the pines on banks of Zozere River in central Portugal, *Sao Pedro* offers its guests simple but comfortable rooms, every conceivable water sport at the doorstep, good food in the dining room and a price that almost defies belief.

Coimbra, 3000 Costa de Prata

Avenida   Double with bath *$25*
Avenida Emidio Navarro 37   Telephone 22156

Modest, but it's close to the middle of this old university town, beside a park along the river. You will find it both comfortable and a blessing to your travel budget. Meals available, but try nearby *Dom Pedro* restaurant on same street.

Astoria   Double with bath *$38*
Avenida Emidio Navarro 21   Telephone 22055

A fine old-fashioned hotel with every comfort, completely renovated in 1982 yet retains a full measure of charm to go with its new look. Please don't miss a visit to the university, one of Portugal's finest and most beautiful.

Elvas, 7350 Planicies

Pousada de Santa Luzia   Double with bath *$32.50*
On E4, just outside town   Telephone 22194

Elvas makes a sensible stop for anyone driving the main Madrid-Lisbon highway, just 10 miles from the frontier. *Santa Luzia* is justly famous for its kitchen, with many Spaniards crossing the border just for a meal here. The old Roman town sparkling in blazing sunlight is a delight to behold.

Estremoz, 7100 Planicies

Pousada da Rainha Santa Isabel   Double with bath *$51.50*
Largo Dinaz   Telephone 22618

On the same Madrid-Lisbon highway, 24 miles west of Elvas, you will find one of the most magnificent Portuguese *pousadas,* built on the site of the old Castle of Estremoz and surely as regal as its forebear. Gleaming tile floors, canopied beds, a dining room to please royalty and regional food that may cause you to extend your visit a few days. The little market town is also a gem.

Evora, 7000 Planicies

Pousada Dos Loios   Double with bath *$51.50*
Largo Conte de Vila Flor   Telephone 24051

It's a tossup for which is the more enchanting, the town of Evora or *Dos Loios*. Both have the flavor of Rome, the Moorish occupation and a touch of the Renaissance running strong in their makeup, and many Portuguese consider Evora a national treasure. We agree and cast a similar vote for *Dos Loios*.

Guimaraes, 4800 Costa Verde

Pousada Santa Maria de Oliveira   Double with bath *$44.50*
Center of town   Telephone 41893

Guimaraes is the birthplace of Portugal and the *pousada* was created from patrician manor houses at the heart of the city. It has its share of other imposing architecture and we recommend a visit.

Lagos, 8600 Algarve

Casa de Sao Concalo   Double with bath *$44-48*
Rua Candido dos Reis 73   Telephone 62171

Fifty miles east of Faro at the tip of the Algarve you will find this small town of weaving cobbled streets and flaming bougainvillea has kept much of the region's original charm. Right in the middle of Lagos, *Sao Concalo,* a former residence, has kept all of it. Just 12 rooms and breakfast only served, but you will thoroughly enjoy the hospitable and homelike atmosphere created by the owners.

Lisbon, 1100

Flamingo   Double with bath *$26-34*
Rua Castilho 41   Telephone 532191

Near the Park Eduardo VII, just off Avenida da Liberdade, the *Flamingo* is everything you seek in a small mid-city hotel. Service is friendly and crisp, modern appointments, small bar and restaurant.

Residencia Inglesa/York House **Double with bath *$48***
Rua das Janelas Verdes 32   Telephone 662435

A 16th-century monastery with additional rooms in an English-style annex a block away, York House is all charm from its stone entryway spilling with flowery vines to the lovely dining room. It's best to take a taxi here as the hotel isn't in the central city. *York House* has been in our book for 20 years and we still love it.

Albergaria Senhora do Monte **Double with bath *$48***
Calcada do Monte 39   Telephone 862846

Another one outside the central city, but well worth the taxi ride. A very homey place with surely the best view of Lisbon and the Tagus River from its nest atop one of the city's hills. Breakfast only and you will feel a part of the Lisbon life-style here.

Marvao, 7330 Planicies

Pousada de Santa Maria   **Double with bath *$32.50***
15 miles N of Portalegre   Telephone 93201

Only nine rooms here, and Marvao nothing if not remote, so please book ahead for this one. Town a fortified medieval enclave watched over by an imposing castle reigning above its red tile roofs and blazing white walls. Regional food served in the *pousada* is sturdy and delicious and you won't forget the piquant local sausage.

Miranda do Douro, 5210 Montanhas

Pousada de Santa Catarina   **Double with bath *$32.50***
Border opposite Spanish   Telephone Miranda 55
city of Zamora

A contemporary and very comfortable *pousada* in a tiny village in this remote area of the country. Balconies overlook the Douro Valley and vineyards for Portugal's renowned Port wine blanket the region. Again, only 12 rooms so make your arrangements early.

Monte Gordo, 8900 Algarve

Albergaria de Monte Gordo — Double with bath *$45*
Avenida Infante D. Henrique — Telephone 42124

A family style and very efficient little place right on the beach with gaily painted fishing boats pulled up almost to its front door. Town near Spanish border and hotel offers respite from the large resort complexes that have sprung up along the Algarve. Dining room serves the best and freshest of local seafood and we heartily recommend a few days relaxing in the sun here.

Nazare, 2450 Costa de Prata

Da Nazare — Double with bath *$35*
Largo Alfonso Zuquete — Telephone 46311

The *Nazare's* terraces and dining room overlook this colorful fishing village that has become one of Portugal's most popular. It's the town's finest hotel and also one of the better places to eat. Fifty rooms, most with glorious views.

Pensao Europa — Double (no private baths) *$26*
Praca Manuel de Arriga 23 — Telephone 46536

Near beach at the heart of town and the 18 double rooms are simplicity itself. It's a short walk to many beachfront restaurants and the *Europa* offers balm to your budget.

Obidos, 2510 Costa de Prata

Pousada do Castelo — Double with bath *$51.50*
Paco Real — Telephone 95105

One of Portugal's most beautiful old walled towns and certainly one of its most exquisite *pousadas,* a rebuilt 15th-century palace with a handsome courtyard and six sumptious rooms. Another place to spend a few quiet days enjoying local food and scenery.

Palmela, 2950 Lisbon Coast

Pousada de Palmela — Double with bath *$51.50*
33 miles SE of Lisbon — Telephone 2351226

Another of Portugal's best *pousadas,* a renovated monastery within a Moorish castle that was only recently opened. It's a marvelous place for Lisbon-only visitors who would like to spend a day or two sampling the countryside.

Porto, 4000 Costa Verde

Grande do Porto   Double with bath *$40-44*
Rua de Santa Catarina 197   Telephone 28176

One of Porto's finest, in the central city with every amenity including air conditioning. Good restaurant and pleasant bar. Have a *porto seco* in the latter. We brought home two bottles of this lovely nectar.

Praia da Rocha, 8500 Algarve

Bela Vista   Double with bath *$46*
3 miles S of Portimao   Telephone 24055

It's difficult not to go into an advanced state of ecstasy over the *Bela Vista,* proof that a perfect jewel doesn't have to be large. Stately fireplaces crowned with magnificent blue Algarve tile, inlaid wood, crystal chandeliers, cozy bar and library, more gorgeous blue tile murals at every turn, yet it still has the comfortable feeling of a private home. We almost forgot to mention the majestic view of what seems to be the entire Algarve coast from its perch above the beach.

Povoa das Quartas, 3400 Montanhas

Pousada de Santa Barbara   Double with bath *$32.50*
4 miles E of Oliveira do   Telephone 52252
Hospital; 49 E of Coimbra

A contemporary place obviously designed to present a spectacular view of the Serra da Estrela Mountains in the distance. Interior colorful, surroundings very tranquil. Only 16 rooms, full dining.

Sagres, 8650 Algarve

Pousada do Infante

                                     Double with bath *$44.50*
                                     Telephone 64222

At the Atlantic tip of the Algarve, *Infante* embodies every characteristic of the region: red earth, almond trees, sparkling white walls and the unique, decorative-only Algarve chimneys. These 18th-century copies of Moorish minarets denote the family's wealth, are painted three times yearly and, of course, never used. Look for them throughout the region.

Santiago do Cacem, 7540 Planicies

Pousada de Sao Tiago   Double with bath *$32.50*
Estrada Nacional   Telephone 22459

Only seven rooms at this small but pleasant one 60 miles south of Setubal. The Atlantic is 10 miles distant, but you have your own swimming pool at Pousada..

Santa Clara-a-Velha, 7665 Planicies

Pousada Santa Clara   Double with bath *$32.50*
Barragem de Santa Clara   Telephone 52250

Only six rooms at *Santa Clara,* in the foothills of Serra da Mesquita on lake three miles southeast of village. Look for the region's excellent smoked ham in dining room.

Sao Bras de Alportal, 8150 Algarve

Pousada de Sao Bras   Double with bath *$32.50*
Mile N on Lisbon road   Telephone 42305

Town seven miles north of Faro in hills above Algarve coast and you'll love the region. Visit the market town of Loule seven miles east of Sao Bras for a tourist-free shopping spree for ceramics, copper and basketwork. The Algarve chimneys on farm houses along the way are captivating.

Sarem, 3750 Costa de Prata
Pousada de Santo Antonio   Double with bath *$32.50*
                                        Telephone 52230

Sarem just off main Coimbra-Porto highway about midway and *pousada* overlooks Vouga River Valley. Lots of hunting and fishing nearby and the inn's beamed ceiling dining room often serves excellent fish and game. Beautiful grounds with fruit trees.

Serpa, 7830 Planicies

Pousada de Sao Gens   Double with bath *$32.50*
Mile S of town   Telephone 52327

Located on Lisbon-Seville highway 18 miles from border where the land has already begun to take on the rolling, dry look of Andalusia. The village of Serpa also has an Andalusian look, with its narrow streets, white buildings and ironwork window grills in the Moorish manner. *Sao Gens* set in grove of cork and olive trees.

Serra da Estrela, 6260 Montanhas

Pousada de Sao Lourenco   Double with bath *$32.50*
8 miles N of Manteigas   Telephone 47150
on Gouveia road

A rustic, ski-resort type inn on the north slopes of Estrela Mountains, Portugal's highest. Huge roaring fireplaces in winter, spacious decks for summer sunning, and roast lamb is a kitchen specialty.

Serra do Marao, 4600 Costa Verde

Pousada de Sao Goncalo   Double with bath *$32.50*
Just E of Vila Real on   Telephone 46123
Amarante road

Located at roadside at the head of a vast pine valley of the Marao Mountains, *Sao Goncalo* is sure to be welcomed by the weary driver in this rugged country. Make certain that one of the 18 rooms is reserved in your name!

Setubal, 2900 Lisbon Coast

Pousada de Sao Filipe   Double with bath *$51.50*
Mile E of city   Telephone 23844

Within the walls of Setubal Castle, the rustic furnishings

and spectacular views of *Sao Filipe* make its 15 rooms always at a premium with visitors. Seafood from the bay below is excellent.

Sintra, 2710 Lisbon Coast

Palacio dos Seteais   Double with bath *$60-80*
Mile W on Colares road   Telephone 2933200

Many claim that when you walk through the regal gateway (looking very much like one of ancient Rome) and enter the hotel, you are in Portugal's finest. We couldn't agree more. Hand-painted walls to resemble wallpaper, antique headboards of carved wood above the beds, tile baths and magnificent flower arrangements every way you turn. An intimate bar, dining room to challenge any in Lisbon for Continental food, yet there are only 18 bedrooms. A stay here is surely good for the soul.

Torreira-Murtosa, 3800 Costa de Prata

Pousada da Ria   Double with bath *$32.50*
On water just N of Aveiro   Telephone 46132

You're likely to feel a part of the ocean, or maybe drop your room keys into it from a balcony, at this modern *pousada* that juts out over the Aviera Lagoon. Just 15 rooms and the seafood is heavenly.

Viana do Castelo, 4900 Costa Verde

Santa Luzia   Double with bath *$45-55*
Monte de Santa Luzia   Telephone 22192

If you stop in Viana do Castelo, by all means stay at this fine older hotel high above the city on a beautifully wooded mountain. Swimming pool, tennis, good dining room and wondrous views. We first found it 15 years ago and still consider it town's best.

Valenca, 4930 Costa Verde

Pousada de Sao Teotonio
On banks of Minho River

Double with bath *$44.50*
Telephone 22252

The Minho marks Portugal's northern border with Spain, so your views are of both countries. Hand-crafted furniture in your room, fish from Minho and the Atlantic and the crisp *vinho verde* wines tingling in your mouth. A marvelous place to start, or finish, a Portuguese visit.

Metropol / Moscow

Russia

Independent travel is possible in the USSR and can be very rewarding, but it takes a bit of doing. First order of business is to contact *Intourist*, the official Russian tourist information office in New York, and ask for their brochure *Visiting the USSR*, which will explain the rather complicated steps in getting a visa, plus other important tips for visitors.

Leningrad is considered Russia's "Continental" city and you will find the atmosphere much lighter here than elsewhere, due in part to its proximity to the Finnish border and Helsinki and its distance from bureaucratic Moscow. It is a beautiful city on the broad Neva River and a visit to its magnificent Hermitage museum alone is well worth the 250-mile drive or train trip from Helsinki. Moscow is also a great city and, while not as relaxed as Leningrad, has the museums, arts, architecture and assorted other sights and attractions to occupy any visitor for three or four days.

You will find yourself in the arms of *Intourist* for much of your stay in Russia, a mixed blessing at best. Their people will meet trains, arrange city tours, get Bolshoi ballet and opera tickets and reel off a litany of glories and benefits of life in the USSR today. But they are both human and necessary, so make the best of it.

SAS and *Finnair* will fly you there from the US; *Air Canada, Finnair* and *SAS* from Canada. *Intourist* will rent you a small, 4-seat *Volga* for about $90 per week plus 15 cents per kilometer driven, no tax. Fuel at this time is $1.10 per gallon, and an International Driver's License is definitely required.

Russian trains can be fairly good on long runs (Leningrad-Moscow is one of the best, particularly at night), but equally as grim for short trips. They of course don't honor *Eurailpass*, but have extensive tours and excursions, booked through *Intourist*, that often combine with motorcoach service. One 9-day, all-rail tour includes first-class hotel accommodations in four cities, all meals, guides, baggage handling, the works, for approximately $380 per person. Inter-urban buses are best used for booked tours only.

Russian currency is the *ruble*, divided into 100 *kopeks*, and therein lies the rub of visiting Russia. The official rate is one *ruble* for $1.35, but the *ruble* sells for less than 40 cents outside Russia, which is academic as you can neither import or export them as an individual. Banking hours are not important since you will buy *rubles* at the official rate in *Intourist* hotels. Your shopping will probably be confined to *Beryozka* "hard-currency" shops (that's any foreign money) in *Intourist* hotels. Most of these hotels also have hard-currency bars open to foreigners only and the vodka flows freely.

Dining in Russia can be a delight or an absolute disaster. Service is invariably slow and frequently surly. Your best bet is to seek out a restaurant specializing in food of one region: the Caucasus republics of Georgia or Armenia, the Ukraine, Baltic or one of her Eastern European friends, Hungary or Bulgaria. And be sure to have your *Intourist* desk make a reservation as waiting lines for the best places are usually long.

Foreigners travel first-class and up in Russia and this will make your stay expensive. But don't try to stretch your funds by accepting the kind offer of a favorable exchange from the friendly taxi driver or young man on the street-corner, unless you'd like an all-expenses, no-choice visit to Siberia as part of your itinerary.

Hotels & Inns

Kiev

Dnipro   Double with bath *$50*
Leninsky Komsomol Square   Telephone 297270

A typical Russian highrise (all 12 stories) on a huge square at city center. *Dnipro* has everything Russia offers in hotel amenities, which means *Intourist* bureau, currency exchange desk, "hard currency" bar, plus dining room food that is both nourishing and filling, when it arrives. Kiev, capital of the Ukraine, is one of Russia's lovliest and most historic cities.

Leningrad

Europa   Double with bath *$70*
1/7 Brodsky Street   Telephone 2119149

Europeyskaya has an excellent location just off Nevsky Prospekt, a main thoroughfare, near the Kirov Ballet Theater. It also has miles of corridors and a main dining room styled to resemble a 19th-century southern or mid-western church, which gave an ecclesiastic flavor to our *chicken kiev*. There is also an official *Beriozka* souvenir shop for buying marvelous enameled eggs or a fur hat. Don't miss this exciting and beautiful city, nor a visit to the Hermitage Museum/Winter Palace, housing one of the world's greatest collections of art.

Minsk

Yubileinaya	Double with bath *$50*
19 Parkovaya Magistral	Telephone 298023

Your only choice in Minsk and it's a good enough version of the modern Russian hotel, where you are forever in the tender arms of *Intourist*. The dining room is capable of turning out good, and colorful, Byelorussian dishes. All rooms here are first class, which is the only way westerners may travel in the country.

Moscow

Metropol	Double with bath *$70*
1 Marx Prospekt	Telephone 2256677

Here is an old-fashioned hotel to take you back to pre-revolutionary days, a marvelous place with dining room right out of Versailles, complete with huge fountain at its center. *Metropol* also has the perfect location for Moscow, a step from Red Square and just across a park from the Bolshoi. There's an international flavor at the *Metropol* that one doesn't find elsewhere in uptight Moscow, so pull every string you have and badger *Intourist* for a reservation here.

National	Double with bath *$70*
14/1 Marx Prospekt	Telephone 2036539

Another older fixture at city center just across the park from *Metropol*. Your room could overlook Red Square and the Kremlin, the bar is lively and we had an excellent meal in the dining room. Rooms aren't as huge as *Metropol's*, but make this your second choice when booking with *Intourist*.

Odessa

Odessa
11 Primorsky Boulevard

Double with bath *$50*
Telephone 225019

Smallest *Intourist* hotel in city, not always a drawback, and it has all the services you need, including a gift shop. Odessa is an industrial city, yet its location near Black Sea beaches, the magnificent Opera and Ballet Theater and impressive Primorsky Boulevard make it a favorite with Russian visitors.

Yalta

Oreanda
35/2 Lenin Street

Double with bath *$50*
Telephone 25794

Yalta lies on the southern coast of the Crimea and it's probably blessed with the country's best weather. Lots of scenic excursions may be booked through the *Oreanda's Intourist* desk.

Suffolk Hall / Edinburgh

Scotland

Scotland is of course a part of Great Britain, but the latter's "Tight Little Island" scale changes almost immediately upon crossing the Cheviot Hills from Northumberland in the north of England. The stone fences and hedgerows separating meadowlands now reach over the horizon in endless ribbons and this spacious and thinly populated land of shimmering lochs and rivers, purple heather and glorious wildflowers is a haven for the traveler seeking quietude along with splendor.

Scotland has traditionally been divided into Highlands and Lowlands, but the only real low country is found in the central valley cinching Scotland's waist between the Firth of Clyde and Firth of Forth, roughly from Edinburgh to Glasgow.

Clans and their tartans form a strong and historic link to Scotland's past, but today's Scotsmen are far from clannish and the welcome here is as warm as you will receive in Europe. Few places in the country are lacking in scenic beauty, from the lonely Cheviot Hills to the wilderness of the Northwest Highlands' Sunderland, but the Spey River valley, Loch Ness and the firths, islands and lochs of the rugged west coast are fascinating to behold. Try mightily to reach this part of Scotland after the obligatory few days in Edinburgh.

British Airways, British Caledonian, Pan Am, TWA, American and *Delta* will get you there from the US, some with stops in London; *Air Canada* and *BA* from Canada. *Hertz* and *Avis* will rent you a Ford *Fiesta* or *Escort* for around $225 per week unlimited mileage, plus tax of 15%. Fuel is now about $2.70 per Imperial gallon, 20% more than a US gallon.

- Scotland's trains do not honor *Eurailpass* but the *BritRail* pass is good for 7, 14, 21 or 30 days with first-class cost for these periods $147, 219, 272 and 317. Second-class is $107, 162, 205 and 243 and either pass must be purchased before you enter Britain. Your nearest *BTA* office will have full information on *BritRail* as well as on bus travel within Scotland, an excellent way to visit the more remote reaches of the Highlands.

The Scottish pound, pegged in value to the pound in England, is currency north of the border and current value is $1.68. Banking and shopkeeping hours are about the same as those of England but pub hours vary. Voltage is again 220 and summer temperatures are usually in the 60s with cool evenings, but winter weather can be awfully raw. Should time prevent your trip extending into the Northwest Highlands, the lovely Trossachs begin only some 40 miles northeast of Edinburgh and you will find gentle mountains, heather and thatched cottages aplenty here.

Scottish food, to a visitor anyway, is not all that different from England's, with perhaps a bit more lamb and Aberdeen's superior beef added to the pot. Fresh fish from the North Sea and Atlantic are invariably good throughout Scotland and haggis, the national dish, is easy enough to find in some form. Scottish bakers turn out a mouthwatering array of breads which the English can't match: soda scones, oatcakes, shortbreads, "baps" breakfast rolls and the like, which always makes breakfast in Scotland an adventurous meal, particularly on a farm.

Cock-a-leekie soup and Scotch broth are staples and smoked salmon here is like none other in the world. Try Ayrshire cheese, similar to Cheddar but moister, or a Scotch egg with your pint as pub fare, and Dundee cake of currants, almonds and glazed cherries will satisfy the sweet tooth in anyone.

Scotland's prices continue to climb and have now reached the point that they must be called expensive. More's the pity!

Hotels & Inns
(Bed and Breakfast)

Balloch, Strathclyde (Dunbartonshire)
Balloch   Double with bath *$38-48*
                                           Telephone (0389)52579
This 18th-century inn on the River Leven at the southern end of Loch Lomond is ideal for the fisherman, having two bodies of water to wet a line. Ten rooms and full meal service.

Banchory, Grampian (Kincardineshire)

Banchory Lodge   Double with bath *$65-75*
17 miles SW of Aberdeen   Telephone (03302)2625

Another 18th-century country house with its own 19 acres.
On River Dee, loaded with trout and salmon, which you may
fish as guests of lodge. Splendid food and chipper service.

Bridge of Cally, Tayside (Perthshire)

Bride of Cally   Double with bath *$35-45*
21 miles N of Perth   Telephone (025086)231

On a hill near the historic old stone bridge, this 200-year-old
inn on the River Ardle has nine rooms and all the outdoor
recreation that goes with its scenic setting: walking, fishing
and easy slopes for winter skiing.

Callander, Central (Perthshire)

Highland House   Double with bath *$30-38*
South Church Street   Telephone (0877)30269

A small hotel of only nine rooms that is family run with
great pride in the kitchen. Fresh fish from nearby lochs and
rivers a specialty. Trossachs to the west are our favorite Scottish mountains, well worth a side journey from Callander.

Dornoch, Highlands (Sutherland)

Dornoch Castle   Double with bath *$41-48*
60 miles N of Inverness   Telephone (086281)216
on North Sea Coast

This 450-year-old former bishop's palace has 18 rooms in
one of its wings. Sutherland is really up there in the Highlands and even a castle seems cozy in this remote area. Fine
food and drink.

Easdale, Strathclyde (Argyll)

Dunmore House   Double with bath *$46*
Half-mile E of village   Telephone (08523)203

South of the popular coastal resort of Oban, you'll find the

Isle of Seil and tiny Easdale may be reached by a bridge over a small backwater of the Firth of Lorn. *Dunmore House* is worth the effort, a pleasant farmhouse with 11 rooms, five with baths, and marvelous home-cooked meals.

Eddleston, Border (Peebleshire)

Cringletie House   Double with bath *$55-65*
2 Miles N of Peeples   Telephone (07213)233

Just 20 miles from Edinburgh this marvelous 19th-century stone mansion is all turrets, gables and bay windows, a bit like something right out of Sir Walter Scott. Sixteen rooms, a 28-acre estate and garden that provides much of the fruit and produce for *Cringletie's* excellent kitchen. Teas a pleasure here.

Edinburgh, Lothian

Old Waverly   Double with bath *$35-68*
43 Princes Street   Telephone ((031)5564648

Right on famed Princes Street with some rooms overlooking Princes Gardens and Edinburgh Castle, this old favorite has a dining room where you may still order Scottish dishes, which first endeared it to us. Lots of locals agree and *Old Waverly* should be your first choice here.

Suffolk Hall   Double with bath *$40*
10 Craigmillar Park   Telephone (013)6674810
Edinburgh EH16 5NE

Another one of those Sir Walter Scott places loaded with bay windows and such. About two miles from Princess Street and its sights, *Suffolk Hall* just received a glowing report from one of our readers. Rooms without baths available at less expense.

Lauriston   Double with bath *$33-38*
9 Lauriston Park   Telephone (031)2299530
Edinburgh EH3 9JA

Less than a mile south of Princes Street, this little 26-room hotel is all efficiency and no-nonsense. Near the university, it has a dining room singularly lacking in frills that offers such specials as grilled herring in oatmeal, haggis with turnips as well as other more earthly fare.

Arden	Double with bath *$35-50*
18 Royal Terrace	Telephone (031)5568688
Edinburgh EH7 5AQ	

Royal Terrace is in the northeast part of city, overlooking a long garden and Firth of Forth. *Arden* is part of a Georgian block of structures and its chief virtue is huge rooms suitable for families. Several good inexpensive restaurants just down the hill.

Fort Augustus, Highlands (Inverness-shire)

| Fort Inchnacardoch Lodge | Double with bath *$48-58* |
| On A82 | Telephone (0320)6258 |

You might draw a four-poster bed at this old hunting lodge at the foot of Loch Ness, a good base for exploring parts of the Northwest Highlands. Full meal service and a bar for that twilight "splash of malt."

Grantown-on-Spey, Highlands (Moray)

| Craiglynne | Double with bath *$45-60* |
| Woodland Terrace | Telephone (0479)2597 |

Several older homes were joined (it happens often in Europe) to form this most comfortable hotel. Cozy lounges, pleasant bedrooms and sturdy Scot food. Grantown is in the green and tranquil Spey River Valley, with all sorts of outdoor activities including winter skiing in the nearby Cairngorm Mountains.

Inverness, Highlands (Inverness-shire)

| Glen Mohr | Double with bath *$34-60* |
| 10 Ness Bank | Telephone (0463)34308 |

A 19th-century stone mansion right on the River Ness with a very fetching informality about it. Short walk into town but the best area to stroll is in the other direction along the river. Lots of regional food and high teas a pleasure.

Dunain Park   Double with bath *$56-78*
2½ miles SW of town   Telephone (0463)30512

A 17th-century country house that must be called special for
its beautiful setting and marvelous feeling of an old home.
The food deserves mention and there is an atmosphere of
total relaxation and well-being.

Kirtlebridge, Lockerbie (Dumfries & Galloway)

Braes Farm   Double (no private baths) *$23*
On M74 just N of border   Telephone (04615)234

A working farm that we shan't forget: warm, inviting and
spotless throughout. It's marvelous for children (2½ or
older allowed) and our young daughter would disappear for
hours. Plan your evening meal here as it's very good and
there are paltry few other options within miles. Cards or telly
with other guests is the big evening event.

Killearn, Central (Stirlingshire)

Black Bull   Double with bath *$38-48*
SW of Stirling in Lennox Hills Telephone (0360)50215

An old fashioned roadside village inn near the Campsie Fells
that puts you within easy reach of the Trossachs and Loch
Lomond. Lovely little village and the inn's garden is a quiet
spot to soak up Central Scotland's quietude over a pot of tea.

Moffat, Dumfries & Galloway (Dumfriesshire)

Moffat House   Double with bath *$42-52*
High Street   Telephone (0683)20039

This fine old stone house with broad lawns is a fixture in
Moffat, a most typical village in the rolling sheep country of
the southern borderlands. Full meal service including high
teas. Moffat a good place to depart the motorway and follow Tweed River Valley road north into the Pentland Hills
and Edinburgh.

Oban, Strathclyde (Argyll)

Great Western
Esplanade

Double with bath $30-46
Telephone (0631)3101

Hardly a small hotel, but treat yourself to a total 19th-century British holiday hotel experience. This stately facade faces the sea almost defiantly. Within, tea time is a ceremony second only to the coronation and your wakeup pot of tea is delivered with Big Ben reliability. Oban has become a bit fish-and-chips tacky, but it's gay with holiday crowds and the best place to catch a ferry for the Hebrides.

Old Meldrum, Grampian (Aberdeenshire)

Meldrum House
11 miles NW of Aberdeen

Double with bath $55-73
Telephone (06512)294

Parts of this fine turreted mansion date from the 13th-century and the same family has owned it for 700 years. Plenty of time to collect the paintings, prints and antiques that give the patina of an old master to the house itself, which sits in its own wooded estate a mile and a half off the A947 road. Only nine rooms and Meldrum House has the feeling of a private home to which you have been fortunately invited. The sort of superior food you would expect.

Perth, Tayside (Perthshire)

Salutation
34 South Street

Double with bath $37-58
Telephone (0738)22166

Said to be the oldest hotel in Scotland, *Salutation* was once the headquarters of Prince Charles Edward Stewart. Locals line up for Sunday dinner here and we soon found out why. Perth is a tidy market town on the salmon-rich River Tay, and from here north the scenery becomes more spectacular.

Strachur, Strathclyde (Argyll)

Creggans Inn
35 miles NW of Glasgow
on S shore of Loch Fyne

Double with bath $55-66
Telephone (036986)279

Between Argyll Forest Park and Loch Fyne, this unpretentious little inn is nevertheless all coziness and good cheer. The countryside is lovely, fine view of the loch and the dining room will reward you with the freshest of local fish and produce. The feeling of rural Scotland will seep into your bones.

Parador Nacional Carlos V / Jarandilla de la Vera

Spain

Every summer hundreds of thousands of Europeans pour through or over the Pyrenees to vacation in this sun-drenched land. The lure of Spain is that it is a non-European country, cut from the Continent for centuries by the geographic and cultural barrier of these same mountains describing its northeastern border. The 700-year Moorish occupation in a sense split Spain's cultural personality again, leaving it with a rich lode of Muslim architecture, music, food, customs, dance and costume to stir in with that of the Greeks and Phoenicians who had come before and the Hapsburgs and Bourbons who were to follow.

Now add the fact that while much of Spain is made up of the dry, flat central *meseta*, this plateau is ringed with coastal mountains and enough inland ranges to make Spain Europe's most mountainous country after Switzerland. The much overworked "land of contrasts" description fits Spain like a glove: misty Galicia, cool mountain passes in Basque and Catalan Spain, torrid Castile, Extremadura and Andalusia, there is climate and topography for every taste.

Iberia and *TWA* will fly you to Madrid from the US, Canadian travelers connecting with both through New York. Spanish currency is the *peseta*, now worth about $.0077 or 130 to the US dollar.

RENFE, the Spanish rail system, honors *Eurailpass* and also has a *Chequetren* 15% discount ticket of its own for multiple purchases for up to six persons, making travel for families or small groups even less expensive. Purchase at any *RENFE* office in Spain. *ATESA* has a fleet of luxury buses plying the regions of major travel interest on 3 to 15-day all-inclusive tours, cost starting at about $55 per day including accommodations and dining. *ATESA, Hertz* and *Avis* will rent you a *Seat 127* (that's their *Fiat*) for about $211 a week unlimited mileage, plus 4% tax, and super fuel now costs about $2.30 per US gallon. Spanish banking hours are 9:00-

1:00 six days, stores open from 10:00-7:00 six days, with some closing Saturday afternoons. Voltage is 220, 50 cycles.

Spain's *paradores* are a bit more than the stuff of dreams; they are a traveler's dreams become reality. While their origins, and the word itself, date back to the Moorish *waradah* or stopping place, the first of Spain's present system of *paradores* was opened in 1928. Today the converted castles, monasteries, palaces, medieval hospitals and convents, along with a number of elegant and modern mountain or seaside establishments, total around 82 throughout Spain.

There is now a US/Canada booking office for *paradores* in New York, owned by the former information director of the Spanish National Tourist Office, and the telephone is (212) 759-5170. Double room prices for this year range from $34 for most 2-star locations to about $42-47 for 3-stars and $47-52 for 4-stars. Check following pages for those you want and call New York office for bookings.

Cocina espanola is about as straightforward as cooking can get. With the exception of *paella*, a colorful saffron rice dish of Valencia, most offerings from Spanish kitchens arrive at table with few embellishments. Meats are grilled or roasted with a minimum of herbal overtones; seafood, with the exception of some dishes in Basque provinces and Catalonia, is given the same simple treatment. Which of course does not mean that Spanish food is tasteless or dull; on the contrary, it is one of our own European favorites. Wines are marvelous, particularly the sturdy reds of Rioja, and the popular Valdepenas add to any meal. And by all means take part in the *tapas* hour, an exercise of bar hopping between about 5 p.m. and 8 or 8:30 to nibble on little delicacies placed on the bar in endless rows. Enough *tapas* and wine will help you survive to the Spanish dinner hour, 10 p.m. or later through midnight.

While the finest Madrid hotels and restaurants now charge prices near those beyond the Pyrenees, Spain is still very much a budget country where your dollar stretches a great distance indeed.

Hotels & Inns

Avila, Avila (Old Castile)

Palacio de Valderrabanos   Double with bath *$36-38*
Plaza de la Catedral 9   Telephone (918)211023

This 15th-century palace stands just before the cathedral's door and has a stone entryway to match its neighbor's. Within, the magnificent blue leaded windows of the lobby, period furnishings and spacious rooms let you know immediately that this was formerly a nobleman's home indeed. Avila's finest, but the *parador* (see listings) is a delight as well. Don't miss Avila; it joins France's Carcassonne as the two most fascinating walled cities of Europe.

Aviles, Oviedo (Cantabrian Coast)

Luzana   Double with bath *$26-32*
Fruta 9   Telephone (985)565840

Large and well-decorated rooms in this one, your best choice in a town on Cantabrian Coast road near Gijon. No restaurant and the street is very busy, but we found it comfortable and quiet.

Barcelona, Barcelona (Catalonia)

Regencia Colon   Double with bath *$32*
Sagristans 13   Telephone (93)3189835

A marvelous mid-city hotel with an excellent location just a block from the cathedral. Watch locals dance a spirited *sardana* in front of the cathedral doors every Sunday morning, a wonderful sight to behold. No restaurant here, but many in nearby Gothic Quarter.

Montecarlo   Double with bath *$31*
Rambla de los Estudios 124   Telephone (93)3175800

Another fine location, mid-way on the Ramblas, Barcelona's main thoroughfare. Breakfast only, small lobby and bar, with ever-helpful Montserrat at the desk. She knows every good Catalan restaurant in town.

Oriente   Double with bath *$31*
Ramblas 45   Telephone (93)3022558

Across the Ramblas from *Montecarlo* down a few blocks you'll find another good one in the same category. Comfortable rooms, although those on front are a bit noisy at night, and the sidewalk cafe is a place to sit and observe Ramblas activity any time of day or night.

Burgos, Burgos (Old Castile)

Espana   Double with bath *$26*
Paseo del Espolon 32   Telephone (947)206340

At the end of a shaded walkway at city center, a short walk to the cathedral and convenient to everything in this historic town of Old Castile where El Cid was born. All meals served here, but there's a good seafood restaurant just around corner. Ask for the renowned local crayfish.

Burgueta, Navarra (Pyrenees)

Loizu   Double (no private baths) *$16*
Unica 3   Telephone (948)760008

Hemingway characters Jake and Bill (*The Sun Also Rises*) went trout fishing in this Pyrenees hamlet between Pamplona and the French border. We can't pin down whether they stayed at the *Loizu* or *Burguete*, just down the main and only street. But *Loizu's* trout *navarese*, stuffed with local ham, borders on the heavenly. Rooms what you would expect in a simple country inn, but we love everything about the place.

Cadiz, Cadiz (Andalusia)

Francia y Paris   Double with bath *$26-28*
Plaza Calvo Sotelo 2   Telephone (956)212318

A good mid-city hotel, but parking is a problem on its small square. *Atlantico,* on beachfront, larger but it's rather aseptic. Have a sherry at *bodega* on Plaza Victoria, then dine on seafood spread on newspapers at a sidewalk restaurant table.

Cordoba, Andalusia

Maimonides   Double with bath *$32*
Torrijos 4   Telephone (957)2223856

Practically inside the mosque, *Maimonides* is a little jewel and the rooms aren't much larger. A step away you'll find two good restaurants, *Caballo Rojo* and *Los Patios,* the first a little more expensive but both serving excellent Andalusian grilled beef.

Cuenca, Cuenca

Alfonso VIII   Double with bath *$24-35*
Parque de San Julian 3   Telephone (966)212512

A modern hotel on a quiet park at center of city noted for its spectacular gorges with houses literally hanging from their rims. Have a meal at *Meson Colgadas,* one of them, and then visit the Spanish Museum of Modern Art next door. It's fascinating.

Denia, Alicante

Los Angeles   Double with bath *$22*
Playa de las Marinas 649   Telephone (965)780458

A quiet place on the beach three miles north of town, with good seafood served in its dining room. Denia a very popular resort and port on Costa Blanca, also a great place to buy rope-soled shoes for a pittance. We stuff our bags with them.

El Escorial, Madrid

Miranda y Suizo   Double with bath *$22-25*
Florida Blanca 20   Telephone (91)8960000

A delightful little town, usually visited on a day-trip from
Madrid for the monastery, but it's perfect for an overnight.
No better place to spend it than *Mirando y Suizo*, a gather-
ing place for locals for its fine restaurant and lively cafe
scene. Most comfortable rooms.

Granada, Granada (Andalusia)

America   Double with bath *$24*
Real de la Alhambra 53   Telephone (958)227471

One of our favorite small hotels in Spain, 14 rooms set
around a central patio for dining, steps from the Alhambra.
The *parador* a few more steps and pomegranate trees just
outside your window! Family run, very good food and reservations should be made for this one.

Guadalupe   Double with bath *$29*
Avenida de los Alijares   Telephone (958)223423

Also on the Alhambra hill, which has most of the sights you
visit Granada to see. Larger, with 86 rooms, and full meal
service available.

Huesca, Huesca (Aragon)

Pedro I de Aragon   Double with bath *$32*
Del Parque 34   Telephone (974)220300

Severely modern and on a pleasant park the whole town uses
for family outings. Hotel the city's best. But try to have an
evening meal at *Meson Quijote*, a popular place near the
cathedral with Aragon's *serrano aracena* hams, Spain's
best, hanging from the ceiling.

Javia, Alicante (Valencia)

Plata   Double with bath *$20*
Playa Montanar 83   Telephone (965)7901050

Right on the beach two miles southeast of town, this is a

place to relax for a few days, enjoy local food and swim in the blue Mediterranean. You won't miss the Costa del Sol's highrise hotels.

Leon, Old Castile

San Marcos   Double with bath *$56-65*
Plaza San Marcos 7   Telephone (987)237300

This regal palace, first built for the Order of Santiago (knights protecting pilgrims on the Way of St. James) in the 16th-century, later served as a hospital and monastery. It still houses the city's archeological museum of rare objects from Roman and medieval times, yet also functions as one of Spain's most luxurious hotels. Superlative regional fare from the kitchen, cathedral-like bar and a facade as imposing as the Elgin Marbles.

Luarca, Asturias

Gayosa   Double with bath *$35*
Paseo de Gomez 4   Telephone (985)640054

Somehow we always return to this fetching little town on the coast and look forward to a stay at *Gayosa* on the main plaza. Cheerful rooms, some overlooking the plaza, others the river, and a fine place to eat next door. Harbor resembles those of Cornwall and it's a joy to walk around town.

Madrid, New Castile

Prado   Double with bath *$37-68*
Calle Prado 11   Telephone (91)4293568

Our favorite Madrid hotel for its location within walking distance of everything in the Old City: Prado Museum, Plaza Mayor, Puerta del Sol, marvelous shopping, good restaurants and just around the corner from a clutch of marvelous *tapas* bars. No full meals, but a small cafe for breakfasts and snacks. Don't miss nearby *El Lacon* restaurant for simple but sturdy Castile food.

Victoria   Double with bath *$40-45*
Plaza del Angel 7   Telephone (91)2314500

Just down the street from *Prado*, and much larger, you'll find the stately *Victoria* with every comfort. It's even closer to city center and has dining room. For excellent Basque food, try the small and modest *Casa Vasca* at Victoria 7, just off Puerta del Sol three minutes from hotel.

Carlos V   Double with bath *$33-54*
Calle Maestro Vitoria 5   Telephone (91)2314100

Dead center of everything is this rather ornate, old-fashioned place with slightly busy furnishings. Rooms are far from huge, but no matter. It's near Avenida Jose Antonia (Gran Via), Madrid's popular shopping street. Don't miss the *Empresa Nacional de Artesania* at #32 with its enormous selection of Spain's finest handicrafts, all for sale.

Gran Via   Double with bath *$38-48*
Avenida Jose Antonio 25   Telephone (91)2221121

Mid-way on the Gran Via and also within walking distance of most sights in the Old City. No restaurant here and there's a good bit of bustle that goes with a mid-city hotel, but readers like the location. Lots of cafes and restaurants up and down the Gran Via.

Jamic   Double with bath *$22*
Plaza de las Cortes 4   Telephone (91)4290068

As modest as they come, but we've been staying here off and on since the 50s and find it very acceptable. Good location, most friendly owners, American Express next door and the *Palace Hotel* bar across the street for five o'clock sherry. Breakfasts only and they're very good. Your budget will love the *Jamic*.

Malaga, Malaga (Andalusia)

California   Double with bath *$24*
Paseo de Sancha 19   Telephone (952)215165

On the edge of central Malaga near the bull ring. Only 26 rooms, all with baths, and the friendliest of owners. The street continues east to the beach at El Palo, about three miles, where you will find several excellent seafood restaurants with tables under awnings right on the sand.

Mijas, Malaga (Andalusia)

Mijas   Double with bath *$36*
Urbanizacion Tamisa   Telephone (952)485800

Would that something good could be said about the Costa del Sol's development during the past two decades. Alas, most of it is highrise and Mijas itself hasn't exactly closed its eyes to the tourist trade. Yet *Hotel Mijas* has somehow kept the best of the old while providing every modern convenience. Tennis, pool, good enough food and comfortably removed from the tour buses that often glut the little town.

Nuevalos, Zaragoza (Aragon)

Monasterio de Piedra   Double with bath *$26*
18 miles S of highway E-2   Telephone (976)849011

Founded late in the 12th-century, this former Cistercian monastery is now a marvel of a hotel — remote, tranquil, Eden-like grounds and every comfort including a pool. Great vaulted hallways the length of football fields, twin dining rooms (one the monks' calafactory), vegetables from its own gardens, trout from ponds on the grounds, most rooms with private balconies. It must be the best bargain in Spain, and we usually stay three nights after planning one.

Puerto Lapice, Ciudad Real (New Castile)

El Aprisco   Double with bath *$16*
Madrid-Cadiz highway   Telephone (926)576150

This wayside inn in La Mancha just drips with *manchegan* atmosphere, so much that you might expect Don Quixote to wander by from the next room. Rustic, lots of antiques about and rooms that are simple but neat. Have a meal at *Venta del Quijote* nearby. Fine food and even more atmosphere. The old wine-cellar bar may be the most charming in Spain.

Pamplona, Navarra (Basque Region/Pyrenees)

La Perla   Double with bath *$24-28*
Plaza del Castillo 1   Telephone (948)211903

La Perla, tucked beneath the arcades rimming Pamplona's main plaza, is at the very center of most activities taking place during the Festival of San Fermin in July. While it's far from the town's best hotel, San Fermin's popularity makes it necessary to book for the festival years in advance. Rooms are large if rather plain, the restaurant is excellent

---

Rascafria, Madrid (New Castile)

Santa Maria del Paular   Double with bath *$38-77*
20 miles E of Segovia   Telephone (91)8693200

A 14th-century Benedictine monastery in the Sierra de Guadarrama mountains that is now a splendid 42-room hotel with tennis, a fine pool, magnificent architecture throughout and a dining room to please the most demanding. Excellent local trout and game, plus an ambience to make you linger over every meal.

Ronda, Malaga (Andalusia)

Reina Victoria   Double with bath *$38*
Jerez 25   Telephone (952)871240

Seldom does a hotel play such a large part in one's appreciation of a town as *Reina Victoria*. Perched on the sheer cliff that gives Ronda its dramatic impact, this traditional hotel has a dining room overlooking the gorge, garden walkways running its rim and a small pool we adore. Food and service are exceptional.

Polo   Double with bath *$26*
Mariano Souviron 8   Telephone (952)872447

A neat, no-nonsense place at town center and just a short walk from bullring (a work of art built in 1785), the gorge and main shopping street. Have a meal at *Don Miguel* by the "new" bridge, or at less expensive *Pedro Romero* by the bullring.

Salamanca, Salamanca (Old Castile)

Gran
Plaza del Poeta Iglesias 3

Double with bath *$45*
Telephone (923)213500

The traditional *Gran*, large and just off spectacular Plaza Mayor, is hands down the city's best. Its *Feudal* dining room mixes medieval decor with classic food, both Spanish and Continental.

Las Torres
Plaza Mayor 47

Double with bath *$20*
Telephone (923)212100

Older hotel right on Spain's most beautiful plaza (with apologies to Madrid) and that's its chief virtue. Many of the modest rooms have balconies where you may observe the nightly pageant below, and the restaurant, a favorite with locals, has very good food at very modest prices. We've been happy here more than once.

San Sebastian, Guipuzcoa (Basque Region)

Maria Cristina
Paseo Republica Argentina

Double with bath *$35-40*
Telephone (943)426770

A turn-of-the-century Grand Hotel on a riverbank in the central city. Lovely old rooms with high ceilings and fireplaces, ornate dining room and an air of bygone royalty everywhere.

Parma
General Jauregui 11

Double with bath *$29-33*
Telephone (943)428893

Only 19 rooms here, but it's along a *paseo* beside the river and convenient to everything. Also has a marvelous view of the sea. Breakfast only.

Londres y de Iglaterra
Zubieta 2

Double with bath *$55*
Telephone (943)426989

San Sebastian's finest with the best location right on most popular beach. Basque food is considered Spain's best and you'll find it done very well at *Casa Nicolasa* and *Patxiku Kintana* in the Old Town.

Santiago de Compostela, La Coruna (Galicia)

Compostela   Double with bath *$29-33*
General Franco 1   Telephone (981)585700

Modern hotel in historic old building a short walk from cathedral. Breakfast only, but there's a small cafe to tide you over. City has been the destination of pilgrims on the Way of St. James since the 12th century, reaching two million a year in the Middle Ages, and it is still awe-inspiring. Alive with Romanesque, Gothic and Spanish baroque architecture, you'll probably extend your visit by at least a day. Restaurant *Alameda* our local favorite.

Segovia, Segovia (Old Castile)

Las Sirenas   Double with bath *$20-26*
Juan Bravo 30   Telephone (911)411897

Best location on pedestrian street near shops and a bevy of excellent restaurants. But plan one meal at *Meson de Candido* beside the town's Roman aqueduct. See also *parador* listing for the relatively new one just outside city.

Seo de Urgel, Lerida (Catalonian Pyrenees)

Cadi   Double with bath *$20-22*
Duque Seo de Urgel 4   Telephone (973)350150

A bright and cheery little hotel just a block from the tree-lined *paseo* at village center. All meals here and you'll like it. See also *parador* listing for Seo.

Seville, Seville (Andalusia)

Inglaterra   Double with bath *$45-67*
Plaza Nueva 7   Telephone (954)224970

A traditional, family owned hotel that has been renovated yet retains the flavor of old Spain with furnishings, artifacts and fine old paintings in the public rooms. Central location and convenient to canvas-covered Sierpes shopping street and its cafes.

Murillo   Double with bath *$28*
Lope de Rueda 7   Telephone (954)216095

Tucked in the heart of the old Barrio de Santa Cruz near the
cathedral and alcazar, *Murillo* is the perfect place to capture
the spirit of Moorish Seville. Lots of good little restaurants
in the barrio, walking a daily adventure and the colorful de-
tail in hotel lobby's ceiling worth a visit alone. Breakfast only.

Dona Maria   Double with bath *$45-55*
Don Remondo 19   Telephone (954)224990

On a little street between Barrio Santa Cruz and the cathedral you'll find this charmer loaded with elegance from lobby to rooftop. There's a pool up top and a fine view of
Giralda Tower, one of city's landmarks. No restaurant but a
modest one next door.

Tarragona, Tarragona (Catalonia)

Paris   Double with bath *$24-26*
Maragall 4   Telephone (977)203340

An older traditional hotel and it's just off Tarragona's tree-
shaded Rambla Nova in the central city. Breakfast only
here. Costa Dorada town a seaside favorite with Spaniards, so
make arrangements before your arrival if it's mid-summer.

Toledo, Toledo (New Castile)

Cardenal   Double with bath *$32-38*
Paseo de Recaredo 24   Telephone (925)224900

Hostal del Cardenal is the former residence of Toledo's
18th-century Archbishop Cardenal and that worthy soul lived
very well indeed. Marble-arches, stunning patio, baronial
dining room, an exquisite garden terrace for summer meals
and a fireplace in every room. Owned by the same Gonzalez
Martin family of Madrid's famous *Casa Botin* restaurant,
Cardenal's ovens turn out the same roast suckling pig and
tender lamb that account for *Botin's* worldwide renown.

Valencia, Valencia (Levant)

Excelsior   Double with bath *$30-34*
Barcelonina 5   Telephone (96)3213040

Medina-bu-tarab, City of Joy, was the Moorish name for Valencia and it's easy to see how this town near the lush fruit and vegetable *huertas* of the Levant came by it. You'll be joyful enough at this very dignified and comfortable hotel near the main plaza. Breakfast only, but the fresh Valencia orange juice poured endlessly makes the meal memorable.

Continental   Double with bath *$32*
Correos 8   Telephone (96)3217218

Another one just off the main plaza with its flower stalls and clutch of sidewalk cafes. Don't miss a walk down the long Plaza del Mercado where merchants spread awnings every morning to offer their produce and wares. Or Spain's National Museum of Ceramics, one of the most enjoyable museums in Europe.

Valladolid, Valladolid (Old Castile)

Roma   Double with bath *$28-38*
Heroes del Alcazar de Toledo 6   Telephone (983)222319

We can't recommend *Roma* enough for its huge rooms, good breakfasts and perfect location a block from Plaza Mayor. Have a Basque or Asturian dish at the small *Astur-Vasco* restaurant on a small plaza just across from the hotel. There is usually an enticing display of the day's specials.

Zaragoza, Zaragoza (Aragon)

Conde Blanco   Double with bath *$25*
Predicadores 84   Telephone (976)441411

Within walking distance of Plaza del Pilar and the cathedral, *Conde* is one of the town's best buys. Breakfasts only, but a small cafe that once got us through a three-day waiters' strike when every restaurant in the city was bolted.

Room Parador Prices

(Double room including breakfasts)

Category

	**	***	****
July 1 - Sept 30	$32.50-37.00	$38.00-47.00	$42.50-61.00
April 1 - June 30 (+ Oct)	$28.00-32.50	$33.50-42.50	$42.50-52.00
Nov 1 - March 31	$28.00-32.50	$29.00-42.50	$38.00-52.00

(Prices may vary for paradors in the same category)

Parador Meal Prices

	**	***and****
Breakfast	$ 2.50	$ 3.00
Lunch or dinner	$ 9.00	$10.00
Full pension	$17.00	$19.00

Spanish Government Owned Lodgings
Paradores/Albergues/Hosterias/Refugios

LOCATION	TELE-PHONE	NAME	CATE-GORY
Aiguablava	(972)622162	P.N.Costa Brava	****
Alarcon	(985)331350	P.N.Marques de Villena	***
Albacete	(967)214290	P.N.de la Mancha	****
Alcala de Henares	(91)8880330	Host. del Estudiante	****
Alcaniz	(974)130400	P.N.de la Concordia	****
Antequera	(952)841740	Alb.Nacional Antequera	*
Arcos de la Frontera	(056)362	P.N.Casa del Corregidor	****
Argomaniz	(945)242200	P.N.Argomaniz	***
Arties	(973)640801	P.N.D.Garpar de Portola	****
Avila	(918)211340	P.N.Raimundo de Borgona	***
Ayamonte	(955)320700	P.N.Costa de la Luz	****
Bailen	(953)372	Alb.Nacional Bailen	****
Bayona	(986)355000	P.N.Conde de Gondomar	****
Benavente	(988)630303	P.N.Rey Fernando II Leon	****
Benicarlo	(964)470100	P.N.Costa del Azahar	***
Bielsa	(974)23	P.N.Monte Perdido	****
Caceres	(927)213012	Host. del Comendador	****
Cadiz	(956)212301	Hotel Atlantico	****
Calahorra	(941)130358	P.N.Marco F. Quintiliano	***
Cambados	(986)171	P.N.del Albarino	***
Canadas del Teide		P.N.Canadas del Teide	**
Cardona	(93)8691275	P.N.Duques de Cardona	****
Carmona	(954)253260	P.N.Alcazar Rey D. Pedro	****
Cazorla	(953)295	P.N.Del Adelantado	***
Cervera del Pisuerga	(988)870075	P.N.Fuentes Carrionas	****
Ciudad Rodrigo	(923)460150	P.N.Enrique II	***
Cordoba	(957)275900	P.N.De La Arruzafa	****
El Ferrol	(981)853400	P.N.Ferrol del Caudillo	***
Fuente De	(942)730001	P.N.Rio Deva	****
Fuenterrabia	(943)642140	P.N.El Emperador	***
Gijon	(985)354945	P.N.Molino Viejo	***
Gomera	(922)871100	P.N.Conde de Gomera	****
Granada	(958)221493	P.N.San Francisco	****
Guadalupe	(927)75	P.N.Zurbaran	***
Jarandilla	(927)98	P.N.Carlos V	***
Javea	(965)790200	P.N.Costa Blanca	***
Jaen	(953)232287	P.N.Santa Catalina	****
Malaga	(952)221902	P.N.Gibralfaro	***
Manzanares	(926)610400	Alb.Nacional Manzanares	**
Mazagon	(955)303	P.N.Cristobal Colon	****
Melilla	(952)684949	P.N.D.Pedro Estopinan	****

LOCATION	TELE-PHONE	NAME	CATE-GORY
Merida	(924)301540	P.N.Via de Plata	****
Mojacar	(951)478250	P.N.Reyes Catolicos	****
Monachil	(958)480200	P.N.Sierra Nevada	***
Navarredonda	(918)1	P.N.Gredos	***
Nerja	(952)520050	P.N.Nerja	****
Ojen	(952)826140	Refugio del Juanar	***
Olite	(948)740000	P.N.Principe de Viana	****
Oropesa	(025)172	P.N.Virrey de Toledo	****
Pajares	(985)473625	P.N.Puerto Pajares	***
Pedraza	(911)15	Host. Pintor Zuloaga	****
Pontevedra	(986)855800	P.N.Casa del Baron	***
Puebla de Sanabria	(988)620001	Alb.Puebla de Sanabria	***
Puerto Rosario	(928)850075	P.N.Fuerteventura	***
Puerto Lumbreras	(958)402025	P.N.Puerto Lumbreras	***
Puertomarin	(982)545025	P.N.Puertomarin	***
Ribadeo	(982)110825	P.N.Ribadeo	***
Saler, El	(963)236850	P.N.Luis Vives	****
Sta.Cruz de la Palma	(922)412340	P.N.Sta.Cruz de la Palma	***
Sta.Maria de Huerta	(075)20	Alb.Sta. Maria de Huerta	****
Santillana del Mar	(942)818000	P.N.Gil Blas	***
Sto.Domingo de la Calzada	(941)340300	P.N.Sto.Domingo Calzada	***
Segovia	(911)415090	P.N.Segovia	****
Siguenza	(911)390100	P.N.Castillo Siguenza	****
Soria	(975)213445	P.N.Antonio Machado	***
Sos Rey Catolico	(056)95-8	P.N.Fernando de Aragon	***
Tejeda	(928)658050	P.N.Cruz de Tejeda	**
Teruel	(974)601800	P.N.Teruel	***
Toledo	(925)221850	P.N.Conde de Orgaz	****
Tordesillas	(983)770251	P.N.Tordesillas	****
Torremolinos	(952)381255	P.N.del Golf	****
Tortosa	(977)444450	P.N.Castillo de la Zuda	****
Tuy	(986)600311	P.N.San Telmo	***
Ubeda	(953)750345	P.N.Condestable Davalos	***
Verin	(988)410075	P.N.Monterrey	***
Vich	(093)241	P.N.Vich	****
Viella	(973)640100	P.N.Valle de Aran	****
Villacastin	(911)107000	Alb. de Villacastin	***
Villafranca del Bierzo	(987)540175	P.N.Villafranca d.Bierzo	***
Villalba	(982)510011	P.N.Condes de Villalba	***
Zafra	(924)550200	P.N.Hernan Cortes	****
Zamora	(988)514497	P.N.Condes de Alba	****

Spanish Government Owned Lodgings
Paradores/Albergues/Hosterias/Refugios

Vardshuset Gota / Borensberg

Sweden

Sweden is the geographic spine of Scandinavia, stretching from less than 100 miles north of Germany to well beyond the Arctic Circle, sharing the rugged winters and spectacular scenery of Lapland with Norway and Finland. Here the adventurous traveler will still find tribes of nomads living as they have for centuries with their herds of reindeer. Outside the few Arctic cities and towns, the dazzling lakes and mountain peaks are totally unspoilt and the area's beauty is overwhelming.

Central and southern Sweden have their lakes, *fjords* and coastal islands as well, and Stockholm, laid out on 14 islands, has been called the "Venice of the North." The

Gota Canal from Gothenburg to Stockholm is the perfect route to follow if you would like a generous helping of the country's lakes and mountains.

Eight million Swedes have a Viking hardiness, the usual Scandinavian concern for cleanliness and order, one of the highest standards of living in the world and, alas, pay tax bills that would curl your hair. They have been called dour, but we find the term out-of-keeping with their nature, certainly not when there is a chilled bottle of *aquavit* on the table and a glorious *smorgasbord* yet to come.

SAS, Finnair, Icelandic and *Northwest* airlines will get you there from the US; *Air Canada* and *SAS* from Canada. *LIN*, the domestic Swedish airline *Linjeflyg*, has a *Swedish Air Cheque* ticket that allows one to make 10 separate flights to any airport in the country during a 15-day period, good from June through August and a real bargain.

Avis, Hertz, Europcar and *InterRent* will charge about $238 per week of unlimited mileage for a Ford *Fiesta*, plus 23% tax. Super fuel is currently $2.20 per gallon.

SJ, Swedish State Railways, honors *Eurailpass* and also participates in the *Nordturist Med Tag* Scandinavian rail ticket plan, 21 days or one month of first or second-class train travel. See Denmark entry for prices. *SJ* also operates an excellent bus service spanning the country, with long-distance express runs in summer.

The Swedish *krona*, divided into 100 *ore*, is currency and it's worth about 13 cents US or 7.69 to the dollar. Banks are open from 10:00-3:00, five days, with some branches in larger cities again from 4:30-6:00. Shop hours are from 9:00-5:00 or 6:00 p.m., Saturdays until noon. Electric voltage is 220. Stockholm weather hovers in the 50s and 60s during summer, but count on freezing temperatures or below from November until March.

Sweden's national dish is really an entire table filled with innumerable dishes. You help yourself by courses and the traditional *smorgasbord* order goes something like this: herring always comes first, fried, marinated, smoked, pickled or in sour cream; then more fish — salmon, eel or whatever; then cold meats and salad of gherkins, pickled onions, tomatoes *vinaigrette* or a combination of these; finally the hot plate of seafood or meat croquettes, omelets, herring *au gratin*, and usually those two national favorites, Swedish meatballs and *Jannson's Temptation*, a casserole of potatoes and anchovies baked in a heavy cream and onion sauce. Another popular dish is ground beef *Lindstrom* laced with capers and chopped beets. It's heavenly.

As hearty as *Jannson's Frestelse* sounds, it is frequently eaten at the start of *smorgasbord*, right after that first jolting glass of *aquavit* taken in one gulp. Some sturdy souls continue to knock back *aquavit* throughout the meal, but prudence dictates switching to beer.

Lodging, dining and other costs in Sweden must be described as moderate to expensive, the *caveat* being, as always, that it takes a bit of planning and restraint to stay in the moderate range.

Hotels & Inns
(Taxes and Service Included)

Bjorkliden, 98026 Norrbotten

Fjallet — Double with bath *$36-42*
Turiststation Bjorkliden — Telephone (08)248360

This one is really up there in Northern Lapland, on the shores of Lake Torne-trask near the Norwegian border and town of Narvik. In addition to 66 rooms there are 80 family cottages here. Full pension available.

Borgholm, 38700 Oland

Halltorp Olands Gastgiveri — Double with bath *$45*
S of town — Telephone (0485)55250

The island of Oland on the Baltic coast of southern Sweden

has always been a vacationland for northern Europeans. It may be reached by bridge from the town of Kalmar. This small and very charming roadside inn is located in Viking country and offers its guests excellent accommodations and hearty food.

Borensberg, 59030 Ostergotland

Vardshuset Gota
18 miles NW of Linkoping

Double (no private baths) *$20*
Telephone (0141)40060

Vardshuset means inn in Swedish and this one is modest but comfortable. Only eight rooms, but there's a restaurant and half-pension is no more expensive than room rates.

Granna, 56030 Smaland

Gyllene Uttern
On Lake Vattern

Double with bath *$35*
Telephone (039)10800

An excellent mid-point stop between Copenhagen and Stockholm that usually proves very festive as it's a favorite place for young Swedes to get married. Resembles an old castle, where you may stay, or in more modest cabins by the lake. The baronial dining hall is right out of King Arthur.

Goteborg, West Coast

Eggers
Drottningtorget
40125 Goteborg

Double with bath *$52-55*
Telephone (031)171570

A massive citadel of a hotel, more than a century old and with rooms decorated in different styles. Busy mid-city location and room rates include breakfasts.

OK Motor Hotel
Kaggeledsgatan 43

Double with bath *$48*
Telephone (031)250450

Motor hotels throughout Sweden and most of Scandinavia are excellent places to overnight, particularly when they have full restaurant, pool and sauna as this one does. Large, with more than 100 rooms.

Helsingborg, Skane

Villa Vingard
Sehlstedsgatan 1
25239 Helsingborg

Double with bath *$36*
Telephone (042)114594

A small hotel of 30 rooms in this popular holiday town. You may take either full or half-pension here. Don't miss Hamlet's castle nearby.

Esso Motor Hotel
Florettgatan 41
25255 Helsingborg

Double with bath *$38*
Telephone (042)151560

You'll learn to count on *Esso* and *OK* when you're driving in Sweden, and who wouldn't look forward to an indoor swimming pool to relax from a day behind the wheel. Full restaurant and 180 rooms.

Karlstad, Varmland

Ritz
Vastra Torggatan 20
65224 Karlstad

Double with bath *$47-54*
Telephone (054)115140

Breakfast only, 62 rooms and of course there's a sauna. Karlstad, on the northern shore of Lake Vanern, is known as Sweden's cathedral city and the Varmland region is a favorite with foreign visitors.

OK Motor Hotel
Hojdgatan 3
65468 Karlstad

Double with bath *$46*
Telephone (054)131000

More than 100 rooms and there's a full restaurant, pool and sauna. Comfort and convenience is the order here.

Leksand, 79301 Dalarna

Tre Kullor
Hjortnasvagen 2

Double with bath *$38-42*
Telephone (0247)11350

This delightful inn on the southern shore of Lake Siljan would be a welcomed stopover for anyone with its beautiful setting, homemade meals and general feeling of well-being. You'll like it.

Malmo, Skane

Anglais
Stortoget 15
21122 Malmo

Double with bath *$49-58*
Telephone (040)71450

Breakfast only and it comes with room price at *Anglais*. Fine location on city's main square and convenient to railway station. Southern tip of Sweden is farm country and Malmo is said to have more and better restaurants than any other city.

Mariefred, 15030 Sodermanland

Gripsholms Vardshus
On Lake Malaren
40 miles W of Stockholm

Double (no private baths) *$30*
Telephone (0159)10040

There are two good reasons for visiting this tiny hamlet: a tour of Gripsholms Castle and a stay at Sweden's oldest inn, a small place with only seven rooms right on the water. It dates from the early 17th century. You'll view the castle from your window and enjoy the finest food and wines in the inn's dining room.

Rattvik, 79500 Dalarna

Lerdalshojden

Double with bath *$45-49*
Telephone (0248)11150

A country hotel with 71 rooms in a lovely setting above the eastern shore of Lake Siljan. Marvelous views of the lake and outstanding food in restaurant or on pension plan, which many guests take since Rattvik is a holiday center. Only about 12 miles north of Leksand on the same lake.

Stockholm,

Kung Carl
Birger Jarlsgatan 23
11145 Stockholm

Double with bath *$55-60*
Telephone (08)221240

A real turn-of-the-century hotel with rooms re-decorated in either period or contemporary furnishings, each with a distinct character of its own. Modest, but you're within walking distance of just about anything in downtown Stockholm: Old Town, shopping, the Strand and Royal Palace. Breakfast only and it comes with room price.

City   Double with bath *$58*
Drottninggatan 66   Telephone (08)222240
11181 Stockholm

Another excellent mid-city address, this one a newly restored and very contemporary hotel that is a favorite with Swedes. *City* also within walking distance of main railway station and Stockholm sights. Breakfast included with rates and there's a restaurant here.

Birger Jarl   Double with bath *$60*
Tulegatan 8   Telephone (08)151020
10432 Stockholm

Large, modern and chosen Stockholm's Hotel-of-Year not long ago for its comfort, service and value. Sauna, indoor swimming pool, cafeteria and breakfast included with room price.

Esso Motor Hotel   Double with bath *$45*
Uppsalav Ulriksdal   Telephone (08)7100460
17166 Solna

Another of Esso's sparkling roadside havens, this one most convenient for anyone arriving at Arlanda Airport. Restaurant, sauna, indoor swimming pool and full bar.

Ornskold   Double with bath *$57*
Nybrogatan 6   Telephone (08)670285
11434 Stockholm

Small with only 27 rooms, downtown, recently renovated and everyone gives it high marks for comfort and service. Breakfast only.

Sunne, 68600 Varmland

Lanmansgarden   Double with bath *$35*
                                        Telephone (0565)10301

This country inn on the shores of Lake Fryken north of Karlstad is so typically Swedish it's hard to believe. Gaily painted furniture and lots of flowers to lift the spirits, tranquil garden and shady trees, the finest of Sweden's country cooking with an accent on seafood and room rates that are a great value for this expensive country.

Tallberg, 79303 Dalarma

Tallbergsgarden

Double with bath *$40*
Telephone (0247)50026

Midway between our inns at Rattvik and Leksand you'll find this delightful group of Swedish-barn-red farmhouses trimmed in white. Lake Siljan is popular winter and summer and *Tallsbergsgarden* has its share of steady clients for both seasons, drawn by a *smorgasbord* table known for miles around and the cozy inn itself.

Siljansgarden

Double with bath *$36*
Telephone (0247)50040

If you've ever longed to stay in a sod-roof Swedish country inn, this is the place. Some of the houses date from the 16th century, but the inn opened about 60 years ago. Room furnishings are a mixed bag of antiques and contemporary, yet the feeling is so undeniably country Swedish that it doesn't matter. Sauna of course and notable dining. There are also ten cottages where, as the English say, you may "self-cater" your stay. Prices for these are considerably less than for the main house.

Tanumshede, 45700 Bohuslan

Tanumshede Gastgivaregard

Double with bath *$40-46*
Telephone (0525)29010

On the Goteborg-Oslo coastal road you'll find this 17th-century guesthouse the perfect midway stopping point. All 29 rooms have baths, excellent dining room, the obligatory sauna and enough of the other amenities to make your stay a most pleasant one.

Hirschen / Langnau im Emmental

Switzerland

It's difficult to avoid the time-worn "picture postcard country" description of Switzerland, because that's precisely what it is. Every part of the four ethnic areas of the country (German, French, Italian, Romansh) has its full share of sparkling vistas, lofty mountains, lush forests and sunny meadowlands. Summer or winter, it's a visitor's delight, a country small enough to comprehend and enjoy without spending interminable hours behind the wheel of a car or staring from a train window, both visually satisfying but time consuming.

Great summer-winter resorts dot the map like leaves on a lawn: Zermatt, Klosters, St. Moritz, Arosa, Davos, Wengen, Saas Fee, Montreux, Gstaad, Grindelwald, the list is endless. But the true fun and adventure of Switzerland is to strike out on your own and discover the alpine village, silent lake or gingerbread farming hamlet known but to you, a few dozen local citizens and perhaps a herd of munching cows nearby. And don't forget to picnic along the way.

Swissair, Capitol and *Pan Am* will take you there from the US, *Air Canada* and *Swissair* from Canada. *Avis, Hertz, Europcar* and *Budget* will rent you a Ford *Fiesta* for about $270 per week unlimited mileage, with fuel price now at the 60 cents per liter level, or $2.26 per US gallon.

Swiss trains are Europe's best, if not the world's, and they honor *Eurailpass*, plus having their own *Holiday Card*, a 4, 8, 15 or 30-day pass that costs $77, 103, 129 and 182 first-class, $56, 71, 93 and 129 second-class. It's good on all trains, many postal buses for reaching remote villages and most lake steamers. Write your nearest Swiss tourist office for their *Holiday Card* brochure, or send them a check with your passport number for the pass you want. It's your ticket to freedom on the rails, roads and lakes of Switzerland.

The Swiss *franc*, made up of 100 *centimes*, is valued at $.45 (2.22 to the dollar) and seems to gain strength daily. While the Swiss have kept their inflation well below most of Europe's, and have also held hotel prices down to a virtual standstill the past few years, they can do nothing about our currency *vis-a-vis* theirs. So please keep in mind that the apparent horror of prices in Switzerland and much of Europe is really the fault of our weak dollar, not European avarice as you may think when viewing the dinner check or hotel bill.

Swiss summer temperatures range widely from the low 50s to high 80s, with winters from the 50s down to sub-sub-zero. Banking hours are 8:15-4:30, five days; stores 9:00-6:00, 4:00 on Saturdays. Voltage is 220.

Swiss regional cooking tends to lean toward the cuisine of its nearest border neighbor, Germany, Austria, France or Italy, yet maintains a character all its own. More notable dishes are the *berneplatte*, a multiple-meat offering every bit as heroic as Germany's *bauernschmaus; raclette*, a toasted-cheese-and-boiled-potato plate; *fondue*; and imaginative treatment of veal in a number of ways. By all means try a

Swiss *quiche* on its home grounds, and the simple *rosti* fried potato cake is a national passion. The quality of Swiss wines, which are best drunk young, will surprise you. But then the country is bordered on the west by France, on the south by Italy, so enjoy it like knowledgeable natives.

With waistline and budget in mind, you might order the *teller* or "plate service" rather than a full portion from the menu. Another tip to remember is that good, substantial food is usually available in railway station restaurants throughout Europe. But even by nursing your budget along with such fiscal shortcuts, Switzerland must be accepted as an expensive country for food and lodging. A must for any European visitor, but definitely costly to all but the hostel and backpack set.

Hotels & Inns
(includes breakfast, service, taxes)

Adelboden, 3715 Berner Oberland

Kreuz   Double with half-pension *$56-64*
Gempler family   Telephone (033)732121

A small house of only 24 beds, family run and the half-pension rates (two meals daily) make it a good value. Many popular resorts require this arrangement during high season.

Appenzell, 9050 Appenzell

Santis   Double with bath *$44-55*
Joseph Heeb family   Telephone (071)872644

This gaily painted chalet is in a town near the German and Austrian borders, not far from Bodensee (Lake Constance). It's in a Swiss region noted for citizens long on humor and short of stature. Cheerful outdoor cafe and excellent food here.

Arosa, 7050 Graubunden

Vetter   Double with half-pension *$65-80*
Frau G. Vetter   Telephone (081)311702

One of Switzerland's most popular resorts summer and winter, so expect to find that accommodations are usually a problem. Frau Vetter is noted for the hearty Swiss food that comes from her kitchen.

Basel, 4000 Basel

Krafft am Rhein   Double with bath *$44-60*
Rheingasse 12   Telephone (061)268877
Basel 4058

Most of our readers comment on the fine location and tranquil nature of the *Krafft*, then go on to praise the helpful staff and marvelous breakfasts.

Berne, 3000 Berne

Gurten-Kulm   Double with bath *$50*
3084 Wabern   Telephone (031)532141

On a mountain just outside town in an old historic building, quiet, great view and noteworthy dining.

Goldener Adler   Double with bath *$44-50*
Gerechtigkeitsgasse 7   Telephone (031)221725
Berne 3011

Old Town location in another historic building and it claims to be Bern's oldest inn. Just 40 beds and full dining available.

Baren   Double with bath *$52-57*
Schauplatzgasse 4   Telephone (031)223367
Berne 3001

On quiet street in center of town near Bundesplatz with Swiss specialties in dining room. Should it be filled, they can book you into the *Bristol* at #10, which they also own. Breakfasts only at the latter.

Chur, 7000 Graubrunden

Stern   Double with bath *$45-50*
Reichsgasse 11   Telephone (081)223555

This inn is three centuries old, but took on a new look about
a decade ago when the new owner upgraded the accommodations and kitchen. Now you will find some of the best
dishes of the Grison region served here, accompanied by
wine from the hotel's own cellar.

Davos, 7270 Graubunden

Alte Post   Double with half-pension *$58-64*
Platz   Telephone (083)35403

A small one of 27 beds right on the main square. Don't
forget that these prices give two people two meals daily, and
the *Post* serves some of the better ones hereabouts.

Meisser   Double with half-pension *$65-75*
Dorfstrasse 7   Telephone (083)52333

Another very pleasant house run by the Meisser family at
village center, yet it manages to remain quiet and peaceful.
Some 40 beds here and the friendliest of welcomes.

Geneva, Geneva

Mon Repos   Double with bath *$48-54*
131 rue de Lausanne   Telephone (022)328010
Geneva 1202

This sparkling contemporary hotel sits on a broad green
park fronting Lake Geneva on the Right Bank. We've visited
it for years and can attest to its cheerfulness and fine service.
A few apartments with kitchenettes for longer visits or
families.

Strasbourg et Univers   Double with bath *$44-52*
10 rue Pradier   Telephone (022)313920
Geneva 1201

Another one on the Right Bank, more traditional in furnishings and feeling. Handsome rooms, small and bright dining

room and a bar loaded with Swiss handicrafts. It also has a few family apartments and is remarkably quiet for its location.

Le Clos Voltaire	Double with bath *$35-42*
45 Bis rue de Lyon	Telephone (022)447014
Geneva 1203	

Voltaire's old home is on the Left Bank just off busy rue de Lyon, but no matter. It's at the end of a long drive from the street, right in the quietude of its own lovely park. The gardens are magnificent and so is the old vine-covered building. Five minutes from city center, parking, and less expensive rooms available without baths. We first discovered this charmer years ago (shortly after Voltaire moved out?) and readers never fail to praise it.

Edelweiss	Double with bath *$57-60*
2 Place de la Navigation	Telephone (022)313658
Geneva 1201	

A short walk from the lake, this one was renovated several years ago and is even more sprightly today. The restaurant misses few Swiss specialties on its menu and the decor itself adds an Alpine flavor. Right on a small square, 40 rooms, some without baths.

Grindelwald, 3818 Berner Oberland

Bellevue	Double with bath *$44-52*
E. Steuri family	Telephone (036)531234

With only 16 beds the *Bellevue* is certainly tiny, but it's open all year and that's unusual for Grindelwald. Full meal service and some rooms don't have baths, at lower cost of course.

Gstaad, 3780 Berner Oberland

Saanerhof	Double with half-pension *$56-66*
Saanen 3792	Telephone (030)41515

One way of beating the high costs of a popular resort like Gstaad is to stay outside the village. *Sannerhof*, in the town of Sannen about two miles distance, is a pleasant garden hotel where you'll be more than comfortable. Swiss hotels of whatever catagory are invariably spotless and have crisp service, just what you'd expect of a people who practically invented the hotel business.

Interlaken, 3800 Berner Oberland

De la Paix
Bernastrasse 24

Double with bath *$43-55*
Telephone (036)227044

Many, many of our readers agree with us on this one, writing long letters of praise for the warm welcome, outstanding food and homey comforts. It's centrally located but also very quiet.

Klosters, 7250 Graubunden

Chesa Grischuna
Family Guler

Double with half-pension $118
Telephone (083)42222

Our idea of the perfect Swiss chalet, with Grison decor and furnishings that can only be called classic. Rooms are a marvel of local woodworking, a cozy and traditional bar with beamed ceiling, flowers everywhere and Swiss specialties prepared and served beautifully in the dining room. All this, including four meals, for about the price of a big-city hotel at home. You'll want to stay forever.

Langnau im Emmental, 3550 Berner Oberland

Hirschen
Birkhauser family

Double with bath *$35-44*
Telephone (035)21517

Hirschen is the only inn in this small village, having first opened its doors in 1467 and gotten its "official" wine license in 1649. The decor and architecture are almost too Swiss to believe, and Marla and Walter Birkhauser have built an enviable reputation for their food and winecellar. After all, this charming *landgasthof* has been a meeting place for locals for 500 years.

Lausanne-Ouchy, 1000 Vaud

Angleterre
9 Place du port

Double with bath *$44-55*
Telephone (021)264145

Right on Lake Geneva in lower town. You may catch the

lake steamer practically at your doorstep for a beautiful cruise. Good restaurant here and others along port, but shun the huge, ultra-modern one on pier in marina.

Locarno, 6600 Ticino

Villa Daniela   Double with bath *$44*
Carmine family   Telephone (093)334158

A tiny place in this "Italian" town at the north end of Lake Maggiore. Breakfast only but nearby places all serve Ticino regional food that is northern Italian. Centrally located and quiet.

Zurigo   Double with bath *$52-65*
Central on lake   Telephone (093)331617

A very Mediterranean feeling, with palm trees outside your window, cafe beneath a shady arbor, geranium boxes on window balconies. Good pasta in the dining room, 25 rooms.

Lugano, 6900 Ticino

Holiday Select   Double with bath *$48-60*
Via G. Zoppi 4   Telephone (091)236172

A modern, mid-city but quiet hotel that has room balconies overlooking the lake. Convenient to railway station. Full meal service, a terrace cafe and hotel sauna.

Ticino   Double with bath *$57-70*
Piazza Cioccaro 1   Telephone (091)227772

In the middle of Lugano's delightful old section, one of our favorites in Europe, and a bit difficult to reach as it's in a pedestrian zone. But you'll discover that this warm and comfortable inn is worth every effort for its charming decor, excellent food and pleasant cafe on the piazza.

Colibri   Double with bath *$57-68*
Via Bassone 7   Telephone (091)514242
6974 Aldesago

For a change of pace, try this hillside hotel on Monte Bre high above town with surely the best view of the lake and

Alps. We found it decades ago and have watched it grow into one of the city's best values. Marvelous pool, flowers about, good dining, lots of parking.

Lucerne, 6000 Lucerne

Baren	Double (no private baths) *$23-30*
Pfistergasse 8	Telephone (041)221063

Across the old wooden bridge from the main part of town you'll find this neat, modern place in a pleasant area of little shops. Breakfast only and budget is the key word here.

Goldener Stern	Double with bath *$40-43*
Burgerstrasse 35	Telephone (041)230891

Perfect small hotel of 15 rooms in main part of city and convenient to railway station. Lake and shopping within walking distance and the Swiss-farmhouse style restaurant will serve you well.

Wilden Mann	Double with bath *$60-76*
Bahnhofstrasse 30	Telephone (041)231666

We were transfixed by the atmosphere and feeling of history one gets on stepping into the *Wilden Mann*. Your room may have a few antiques and the dining room is hands down one of the city's best. There's a comfortable-Swiss-burgher feeling throughout and you won't forget this one.

Montreaux, 1820 Vaud

Villa Tilda au Lac	Double with bath *$40-50*
Quai Vern	Telephone (021)613814

An older place, very small, but it's on the lake and convenient to most of the town including railway station. Quiet, small garden, and rooms without baths are less expensive. Breakfast only.

Le Chateau	Double with bath *$34*
1844 Villeneuve	Telephone (021)601357
6 miles S of Montreaux	

In a lakeside village down the shore from Montreaux, this small and very quiet hotel in a historic building offers full meal service and accommodations at prices Montreaux can't match. All rooms with baths.

Murren, 3825 Berner Oberland

Alpenruhe — Double with bath *$54-68*
Telephone (036)552738

About 12 miles into the valley below Interlaken, this charming resort village is beyond Wengen. *Alpenruhe* has fine sun deck, good restaurant and is short walk from ski lifts. One of few in village open year-round.

Pontresina, 7504 Graubunden

Steinbock — Double with half-pension *$78-84*
Walther family — Telephone (082)66371

Pontresina once got the overflow from nearby St. Moritz but now has its own loyal following. Lovely setting, tennis and one of two hotels in town open all year. *Steinbock's* dining room makes the pension plan a very good idea and value.

Saas-Fee, 3906 Wallis

Soleil — Double with half-pension *$53-68*
Telephone (028)571233

Soleil is a fixture in one of the fastest growing resorts in Switzerland and it's still one of the town's better values. We've always been partial to this valley not far from Zermatt.

Mischabel — Double with half-pension *$60-75*
Telephone (028)572118

A colorful, family run chalet near town's parking area (no cars allowed in village). Almost every room with private balcony for sunning and enjoying the spectacular scenery. Don't forget that rates include four meals daily.

St. Moritz, 7500 Graubunden

Sonne — Double with bath *$53-63*
Telephone (082)33527

Excellent value for this very expensive town and they have

rooms without baths (never a problem in Switzerland). The *Sonne's* restaurant/grill is very popular with locals, which is always a good sign.

Steffani	Double with half-pension *$100-140*
Postplatz	Telephone (082)22101

Steffani's prices are still mid-range for St. Moritz. More than 100 years old, it's a fixture at village center and exudes a Grison style in every nook and cranny. Particularly charming are the lounges and dining areas.

Zermatt, 3920 Wallis

Hotel Julen und	Double with half-pension *$90-115*
Dependance	Telephone (028)672481

Several hotels in Zermatt are owned by members of the Julen family, so when writing use full name above. With the Matterhorn through your window and marvelous fondue on the table, you're not likely to forget your stay here. The village is absolutely idyllic (no cars!) and so are the surrounding meadows and woods. Just the place to take a picnic lunch, then nap in the sun an hour or so.

Zurich, 8000 Zurich

Limmathaus	Double with bath *$43-49*
Limatstrasse 118	Telephone (01)425240
Zurich 8031	

Another good central location near Limmat River and not far from the lake. We continue to hear favorably from readers about hotel and its dining room.

Poly	Double with bath *$38-54*
Universitatstrasse 63	Telephone (01)362944
Zurich 8006	

The Huni family has made this small place in the old university section a haven for many *Passport* readers through the years. It's the essence of a Swiss family style hotel, from spotless housekeeping to solid Swiss food in the dining room. Convenient to Zurich's railway station.

Carlton Annex / Yenikoy

Turkey

Turkey comes by its exotic nature naturally, since all but a tiny portion of its land mass is in Asia and it wasn't until 1923 that Kemal Ataturk introduced western ways with the fall of the once-powerful Ottoman Empire after World War I. Ankara, the capital, is on the central Anatolia plain in Asian Turkey, and oriental cultural influences still dominate in a country that is 99 per cent Moslem. Both European and Asian Turkey are more than liberally sprinkled with sites of historic importance to early Christianity, particularly the Aegean and southern Mediterranean coasts. Yet most foreign visitors confine their stay to Istanbul, with perhaps a day-trip boat ride up the Bosphorus for lunch in a village near the Black Sea or a quick taxi trip or ferry over to Uskudar just across the Bosphorus for a taste of Asian Turkey.

Istanbul, at the confluence of the Golden Horn, Bosphorus and Sea of Marmara, boasts one of the world's most spectacular settings. More than 500 mosques dot the city, most of them in the old quarter across Galata Bridge south of the Golden Horn, and countless cupolas and minarets give the city a fascinating skyline. Topkapi and Dolmabahce palaces, the basilica of St. Sophia, the Sultan Ahmet "Blue Mosque" and Istanbul's unique covered bazaar, each is more than worthy of a visit.

Pan Am flies to Istanbul from New York. *Air Canada* flights to any major European capital will connect with a *Turkish Airlines (THY)* flight direct to Istanbul or Ankara and *THY* has a 6 to 30-day excursion ticket for domestic travel. *Hertz* and *Avis* will rent you a *Murat (Fiat) 131* or small *Renault* for about $225 per week unlimited mileage and fuel for it at this writing is $3.50 per gallon, but Turkey has a severe energy shortage and this price is sure to rise. An International Driver's License is required for foreigners.

Turkish railways do not honor *Eurailpass* but they are very inexpensive. They are also rather slow and we would recommend taking only first-class accommodations. Bus travel in Turkey can't be highly recommended and *Turkish Maritime Lines* ships along both coasts of the Sea of Marmara, the Aegean and southern Mediterranean coasts are certainly preferable.

Turkey's currency is the *lira*, divided into 100 *kurus*, and it is now worth .00568 cents or 176 to the US dollar. Banks are open from 8:30-12:00 and again 1:30-5:00, five days and stores usually from 9:00 a.m. to 7:00 in the evening. Voltage is 220, 50 cycles. Istanbul's summer weather is in the 70s and 80s, winters in the 40s and 50s, but central Turkey is usually hotter or colder, depending on the season.

Turkish cooking is as colorful and exotic as the country itself. Middle Eastern spit-grilled *kebabs* are on every menu, almost always of lamb, and they are delicious. The *doner kebab* is almost as popular, thin slices of lamb packed onto a vertical spit beside the fire, then cut to order from the turning rod. Eggplant is prepared in any number of ways, the most popular being braised with tomatoes and onions in a dish called *Iman bayildi* (the Iman fainted) and *karniyarik*, stuffed with minced meat. *Dolmas* of grape leaves stuffed with rice, pine nuts and raisins or currants are seen as often as they are in Greece. Grilled swordfish is delectable in Turkey as is the Mediterranean *barbunya*, a delicate and difficult to eat small snapper. Thick Turkish coffee and the potent *raki* come close to being national drinks.

Turkey is one of the few remaining truly budget countries left for the dollar-wise visitor.

Hotels & Inns

Ankara, Central Anatolia

Dedeman   Double with bath *$42*
Buklum Sokak 1   Telephone (041)171100

Large and first-class is a sensible approach for booking hotels in Turkey and this one fills the bill on both counts. *Dedeman* also has a pool and nightclub where you are sure to see a belly dancer sooner or later.

Kent   Double with bath *$41*
Mithatpasa Cad. 4   Telephone (041)184220

Kent about half the size of *Dedeman* with 120 rooms, but it's still one of the capital's better hotels, first-class in every respect. Ankara is a relatively modern city, but don't miss the Old Town with its medieval citadel, mosque and bazaar.

Antalya, Mediterranean Coast

Antalya   Double with bath *$42*
Fener Cad. Hasim Iscan Mah.   Telephone (03111)5600

Antalya is the city's best, a 150-room modern hotel perched on a rocky cliff at water's edge. There's a pool, small garden and many of the rooms have sea views. *Antalya's* dining room is considered one of the best places to eat in this town on Turkey's Turquoise Coast.

Bursa, Marmara Region

Celik Palas   Double with bath $35
Cekirge Cad. 79   Telephone (0241)19600

If you're off on a Turkish rug expedition, Bursa is the place to find them and *Celik Palas* as good as you'll find to overnight. There's a pool and very good restaurant here also.

Istanbul

Divan   Double with bath $59
Cumhuriyet Cad. 2, Harbiye   Telephone (011)464020

Divan is in the "newer" Beyoglu section of Istanbul, across the Golden Horn from old Constantinople where most of the mosques, Topkapi Palace and the Grand Bazaar are located. Yet you're on a main thoroughfare with lots of restaurants, shops and airline offices. Hotel near Taksim Square is one of the city's best, with every amenity, an elegant restaurant for Turkish and Continental food, plus welcomed air conditioning for summer months.

Park   Double with bath $50
Gumussuyu Cad. 6, Taksim   Telephone (011)436010

A fixture in Istanbul and an old favorite of ours for the great views of Bosphorus and city's skyline from its dining terrace. Still known as the "British Park" by some old timers, it takes pride in its dining room and service. Older, but still comfortable in every respect.

Pera Palas   Double with bath $51
Mesrutiyet Cad. 98, Tepebasi   Telephone (011)452230

Another old standby at the heart of Beyoglu, getting a little long in the tooth these days but still acceptable. Good dining room and you may want to try those of other hotels in the area.

Buyuk Tarabya   Double with bath $65
Tarabya Bay   Telephone (011)621000

About half-way up the Bosphorus toward Black Sea on European side (a half-hour drive) you'll find this ultramodern lap of luxury right on the water. Numerous ferries ply the waterway and you may take one down to the city, up to the Black Sea or across to villages on the Asia side. Everything you need is right here, including exceptional dining and spectacular views from most rooms. One of Istanbul's best restaurants, *Abdullah*, is above the village of Emirgan just a ferry stop or two south of Tarabya on the European side.

Izmir, Aegean Coast

Buyuk Efes   Double with bath *$60*
Cumhuriyet Mey.   Telephone (051)144300

Once known as Smyrna, Izmir is the country's second-largest tourist center and its sandy white beaches have been developed to accommodate the fact. Yet the city and area are archeological wonders of the Roman and early Christian eras. *Buyuk Efes* is Izmir's best, with pool, a couple of fine restaurants and surrounded by a lovely park. Every inch a luxury hotel.

Kismit   Double with bath *$47*
1377 Sok.9   Telephone (051)144385

First-class with most of the conveniences. Also has gardens and dining room, the latter good with the coast's fresh seafood.

Kusadasi, (Aydin), Aegean Coast

Tusan   Double with bath *$39*
31 'ler Mevkii   Telephone (06311)9471/1094

Kusadasi, a little port town that mixes the old with the new, is landing for the many cruise ship passengers making a quick visit to Ephesus (Efes) a few miles inland, once a city of 300,000 and still Turkey's most important archeological site. Ephesus played a major role in early Christianity as St. Paul visited to convert Ephesians still worshipping the goddess Artemis. Later St. John visited the Greek city accompanied by the Virgin Mary, who is said to have died in a small house nearby. *Tusan*, just outside Kusadasi, has its own beach and dining room.

Imbat   Double with bath $39
Kadinlar Denizi Meukii   Telephone (06311)85

Imbat is also just outside the village with private beach. We spent much of our time in Kusadasi wandering in and out of the tempting shops and drinking marvelous Turkish coffee. Results: two-foot-long skewers, hammered out by a local blacksmith, for grilling lamb at home, plus enough of those little brass coffee pots to serve the sultan's armies.

Yenikoy, (Istanbul)

Carlton Annex   Double with bath $60-70
On Bosphorus   Telephone (011)621020

Nine miles above Istanbul on the European side of the Bosphorus, this rather large hotel is blessed with a 34-room annex by the swimming pool. Every comfort, excellent food and a stunning view across to Asia in main hotel dining room.

Palace / Hvar

Yugoslavia

Yugoslavia, once the budget Balkan playground of knowledgeable Europeans, still has all the appeal it has enjoyed for the past three decades, only now the budget price tag doesn't fit quite so comfortably. Still, every inch of the Adriatic coast from the Istra peninsula down through Dalmatia to the Albanian border is lapped by incredibly clear blue water, the towns of Pula, Rijeka, Dubrovnik, Budva and Sveti Stefan just as charming as ever and the sparkling sand and pebble beaches still lined with sun seekers from the four corners of the Continent. Inland, Yugoslavia has terrain for every taste: no forest is greener or thicker than those of Ljubljana Gap in Slovenia; Croatia's lakes and waterfalls near Plitvice are world famous; the Djerdap gorge near the Danube on Romania's border is equally renowned; the verdant Morava River valley with its monasteries yet another contrasting stretch of scenery.

JAT, the Yugoslvian airline, will get you there from the US, but Canadians must fly to a mutual Canadian airline-*JAT* destination city in Western Europe. *Kompas-Hertz, Autotehna* and *Centroturist* are three car rental firms and they will give you a *Renault 4* for about $240 a week unlimited mileage, plus 15% tax. Super fuel is around $2.24 per US gallon, but there are coupons available to visitors at border crossings that give you a 27% discount.

Yugoslav railways don't honor *Eurailpass* but have their own domestic passes available locally. With the drastic devaluation of the *dinar* it is almost impossible to keep abreast of costs for these passes and we can only advise you to contact the Yugoslav National Tourist Office in New York for whatever rail transportation brochures they have. We would advise first-class rail travel.

Just about every Yugoslav village can be reached by bus service, but buses are usually crowded. Fares are considerably cheaper than first-class rail, the 325-mile Ljubljana-Belgrade trip costing about $10.

The *dinar* is Yugoslav currency, currently worth about .016 or almost 63 *dinari* to the US dollar. Banks are open from 7:00 a.m. until noon, six days, and shops from 9:00 a.m. until 8:00 p.m., six days, with some taking a mid-day break of about two hours. Voltage in the country is 220, 50 cycle.

A visa is required for Yugoslavia, obtainable free from Yugoslav embassies and consulates in the US and Canada or at border crossings for a nominal charge. There is also a 30-day tourist entry permit available at border crossings, granted upon showing your passport and paying about 25 cents, but it cannot be extended. Summer months' temperature in Belgrade hover in the 70s, winters usually very nippy in the 30s, but coastal cities are a bit warmer.

Yugoslavian cooking is bedrock Balkan, meaning lots of grilled meats, particularly lamb, plus garlic, onions and peppers. The latter range from mild to the hot-rivet variety, best tried with a glass of cold beer at hand. *Cevapcici* comes as close as any to being the national dish, spicy little beef and pork meatballs often grilled on short reeds or sticks. *Raznjici* are bits of meat given the same treatment and they somehow taste better when bought from a street vendor. Adriatic seafood is excellent and plentiful and so are the country's red wines. Try the grape leaves stuffed with rice and bits of meat, *a la Grec*, and the *sarena* stuffed cabbage is delicious. With potent *slivovitz* plum brandy you're on your own, but equally strong Slavic coffee will help with recovery.

Yugoslavia is no longer rock-bottom and we rate lodging as moderate to expensive by today's European standards.

Hotels & Inns
(Includes Service)

Belgrade, Serbia

National   Double with bath *$40*
Bezanyska   Telephone (011)6011122
11070 Belgrade

This old favorite holds up very well. Breakfast included and there's a small bar. Try the *prsut* (smoked ham) or *sarma*, cabbage stuffed with meat and rice, in the dining room.

Slavija   Double with bath *$42*
Svetog Save 9   Telephone (011)450842
11000 Belgrade

One of the city's largest and a good value in expensive Belgrade. The smaller annex is much more costly, so specify that you want a room in the main hotel if your budget is tight.

Dubrovnik, 5000 Dalmatia

Splendid
Masarykov put

Double with bath *$36-46*
Telephone (050)24733

A small place right on beach in a wooded setting. All 61 rooms have baths and there's a lovely dining terrace beneath the trees with views of the Adriatic.

Neptun
Babin Kuk 1

Double with bath *$32-40*
Telephone (050)23755

Most of the rooms here have balconies overlooking the sea and it also has a pool. Private beach, entertainment in the evenings and the *Neptun's* dining room holds its own for a resort hotel.

Grand Imperial
M.Simon 2

Double with bath *$48-68*
Telephone (050)23688

Unlike the others above, *Grand Imperial* is right in town yet walking distance to beach. An older hotel with traditional furnishings and beautiful lounges. The garden restaurant is delightful. Our favorite and we're sure you'll like it.

Jadran
Miliciceva 1

Double with bath *$37-40*
Telephone (050)23322

Another older place, which in Yugoslavia today means smaller. This one just a step from Lapad Bay, Dubrovnik's main beach, with a cheerful dining room, neat bedrooms and balconies for a private *aperitivo* hour as the sun sets over the bay.

Lapad
Lapad Bay

Double with bath *$38-42*
Telephone (050)23473

A mile and a half from city center, the *Lapad* captures the real feeling of old Dubrovnik, a city that in many ways out Venices Venice. There's a charming garden restaurant here and the beach is but a short stroll away. Dubrovnik's street markets are among the most colorful in Europe.

Hvar, 58450 Croatia

Palace
Hvar Town

Double with bath *$45-55*
Telephone (058)74306

Hvar Island is just off the coast between Dubrovnik and Split and the *Palace's* Renaissance architecture alone is worth a stay here. Sea-water swimming pool, marvelous terrace, excellent fresh Adriatic seafood in dining room and a feeling of total comfort about the place. Right on town port.

Delfin
On beach

Double with bath *$38-45*
Telephone (058)74168

Delfin just the opposite of *Palace*, a modern hotel with spacious terraces, indoor-outdoor dining and 57 rooms with contemporary furnishings.

Ljubljana, 61000 Slovenia

Slon
Titova 10

Double with bath *$38-40*
Telephone (061)24601

Good central location and an excellent layover point when driving through the lush pine forests of Ljubljana Gap to or from Austria. Readers have always liked the *Slon* and so do we.

Opatija, 51410 Crotia

Belvedere

Double with bath *$36-48*
Telephone (051)712433

Belvedere has two annexes, both less expensive than the main hotel. Plan on lots of Northern Europeans at this resort city between mountains and sea.

Kristal

Double with bath *$36-48*
Telephone (051)711333

Everything you would expect in a resort hotel: pool, beach, bar, nightly entertainment. Prices drop drastically during off-season along the Adriatic coast. All rooms with bath and there's full dining at *Kristal*.

Porec, 52360 Crotia
Albatros
Zelena Laguna

Double with bath *$31-34*
Telephone (053)31411

Porec, a collection of small bays on the Adriatic south of Trieste, has always been a bargain, probably due to the endless selection of hotels. Most *Albatros* rooms have balconies overlooking the bay and it's a short walk to water. You'll find every sort of water sport around Porec, plus numerous nude beaches.

Portoroz, 66320 Slovenia
Palace
Obala 45

Double with bath *$53-58*
Telephone (066)73341

Marvelous old resort hotel, very traditional, on Gulf of Trieste just 100 miles east of Venice. We've always enjoyed this stately white mansion near water. There's a private beach and pool, not a bad idea considering how crowded the area gets in summer.

Primosten, 69202 Serbia
Adriatic-Raduca
Outside village

Double with bath *$40*
Telephone (059)70022

A tiny and very charming fishing village on the coastal road 35 miles above Split, Primosten appears on few maps. Adriatic-Raduca is the smallest of a three-hotel group, all with the same name. *Adriatic-Slava* and *Zora* are a few dollars more and have air conditioning, but you'll be happy at *Raduca*. All three share a pine-laden peninsula jutting out from the village.

Rijeka, 51000 Crotia
Jadran

Double with bath *$28*
Telephone (051)421600

The Adriatic is right under your balcony at the *Jadran*, so close you could drop a teaspoon into the water. We first stayed here in the 50s and return as often as possible. Indoor salt-water pool, marvelous food and very much a bargain.

Split, 58000 Croatia

Bellevue

Double with bath *$45*
Telephone (058)47175

An older hotel, but it's one of the smaller ones in town and small places are hard to find in Yugoslavia these days. All of the amenities.

Zagreb, 41000 Croatia

Palace
Strossmajerot 10

Double with bath *$42-48*
Telephone (041)449211

A marvelous medieval city that remains both a cultural center and marketplace, with lots of trade fairs that often make hotel reservations a problem. For a down-to-earth look at commerce today, be sure and visit the old Dolac Market. You can't leave without buying something. The *Palace* is almost a rarity in booming Yugoslavia, a traditional hotel that seems a bit fussy at first, but it grows on you. A welcomed relief from those Pentagon-like bastions of today's mass tourism.

NATIONAL TOURIST OFFICES

Austrian Tourist Office
545 Fifth Ave., N.Y. 10017
3440 Wilshire, Los Angeles 90010
200 E. Randolph Dr., Chicago 60601
1007 N.W. 24th Ave., Portland 97210
736 Granville St., Vancouver V6Z 1J2
2 Bloor St. E., Toronto M4W 1A8

Belgian Tourist Office
745 Fifth Ave., N.Y. 10151
5801 Ave. Monkland, Montreal H4A 1G4

British Tourist Authority
680 Fifth Ave., N.Y. 10019
875 N. Michigan Ave., Chicago 60611
612 S. Flower St., Los Angeles 90017
409 Granville St., Vancouver V6C 1T2
151 Bloor St. W., Toronto M5S 1T3

Czechoslovak Travel Bureau
CEDOK
10 E. 40th St., N.Y. 10016

Danish Tourist Board
75 Rokefeller Plaza, N.Y. 10019
Box 3240, Los Angeles 90028
Box 339, Toronto M5W 1C2

French Tourist Office
610 Fifth Ave., N.Y. 10020
645 N. Michigan Ave., Chicago 60611
9401 Wilshire, Beverly Hills 90212
Box 58610, Dallas 75258
372 Bay St., Toronto M5H 2W9

German Tourist Office
630 Fifth Ave., N.Y. 10020
104 S. Michigan Ave., Chicago 60603
700 S. Flower St., Los Angeles 90017
Box 417, Montreal H5A 1B8

Greek Tourist Office
645 Fifth Ave., N.Y. 10022
168 N. Michigan Ave., Chicago 60601
611 W. Sixth St., Los Angeles 90017
2 Place Ville Marie, Montreal H3B 2C9

Hungarian Travel Bureau
IBUSZ
630 Fifth Ave., N.Y. 10020

Irish Tourist Board
590 Fifth Ave., N.Y. 10036
230 N. Michigan Ave., Chicago 60601
681 Market St., San Francisco 94105
69 Yonge St., Toronto M5E 1K3

Italian Tourist Office
630 Fifth Ave., N.Y. 10111
360 Post St., San Francisco 94108
500 N. Michigan Ave., Chicago 60611
3 Pl. Ville Marie, Montreal

Luxembourg Tourist Office
One Dag Hammarskjold Plaza,
New York 10017

Netherlands Tourist Office
576 Fifth Ave., N.Y. 10036
681 Market St., San Francisco 94105
P.O. Box 19, Toronto, Ontario M5G 1Z3
850 Hastings St., Vancouver V6C 1E1

Portuguese Tourist Office
548 Fifth Ave., N.Y. 10036
919 N. Michigan Ave., Chicago 60611
3440 Wilshire Blvd., Los Angeles 90010
390 Bay St., Toronto M5H 2Y2

Scandinavia Tourist Office
(Denmark, Norway, Sweden, Finland)
75 Rockefeller Plaza, N.Y. 10019

Spanish Tourist Office
665 Fifth Ave., N.Y. 10022
1 Hallidie Plaza, San Francisco 94102
5085 West Heimer, Houston 77056
845 N. Michigan Ave., Chicago 60611
60 Bloor St., Toronto M4W 3B8

Swiss Tourist Office
608 Fifth Ave., N.Y. 10020
104 S. Michigan Ave., Chicago 60603
250 Stockton St., San Francisco 94108
Box 215, Toronto M5L 1E8

Turkish Information Office
821 United Nations Plaza, N.Y. 10017

U.S.S.R. (Intourist)
630 Fifth Ave., N.Y. 10020

Yugoslav Tourist Office
630 Fifth Ave., N.Y. 10111

US/CANADIAN REPRESENTATIVES FOR EUROPEAN RAILROADS

Belgian National Railroads
745 Fifth Avenue
New York, NY 10150

BritRail Travel International
630 Third Avenue
New York, NY 10017

510 West Sixth Street
Los Angeles, CA 90014

333 North Michigan Avenue
Chicago, IL 60601

55 Eglinton Avenue East
Toronto M4P 1G8

409 Granville Street
Vancouver V6C 1T2

French National Railroads
610 Fifth Avenue
New York, NY 10020

9465 Wilshire Boulevard
Beverly Hills, CA 90212

11 East Adams Street
Chicago, IL 60603

2121 Ponce de Leon Boulevard
Coral Gables, FL 33134

360 Post Street
San Francisco, CA 94108

1500 Stanley Street
Montreal H3A 1R3

409 Granville Street
Vancouver V6C 1T2

German Federal Railroad
747 Third Avenue
New York, NY 10017

625 Statler Office Building
Boston, MA 02116

104 South Michigan Avenue
Chicago, IL 60603

1121 Walker Street
Houston TX 77002

10100 Santa Monica Boulevard
Los Angeles, CA 90067

1 Hallidie Plaza
San Francisco, CA 94102

800 E. Girard Avenue
Denver, CO 80231

45 Richmond Street West
Toronto M5H 1Z2

Italian State Railways
666 Fifth Avenue
New York, NY 10019

5670 Wilshire Boulevard
Los Angeles, CA 90036

756 Route 83, Suite 105
Bensenville, IL 60106

2055 Peel Street, Suite 102
Montreal H3A 1V4

111 Richmond Street W., Suite 419
Toronto M5H 2G4

Netherlands Railways
576 Fifth Avenue
New York, NY 10036

681 Market Street, Suite 2108
San Francisco, CA 94105

1 Dundas St. Suite 2108
West Toronto M5G 1Z3

850 W. Hastings Street, Suite 207
Vancouver V6C 1E1

Swiss Federal Railways
608 Fifth Avenue
New York, NY 10020

250 Stockton Street
San Francisco, CA 94108

104 South Michigan Avenue
Chicago, IL 60603

Eurail Information

Trains
Box M
Staten Island, NY 10305

Eurailpass Distribution Center
Box 300
Station R
Montreal H2S 3K9

	Amsterdam	Athens	Barcelona	Belgrade	Berlin	Brussels	Budapest	Calais	Geneva	Istanbul	Copenhagen	Lisbon	Luxembourg	Madrid	Marseilles	Milano	Munich	Oslo	Paris	Prague	Rome	Stockholm	Vienna	Zurich
Amsterdam	—	2929	1505	1786	665	220	1401	392	1236	2740	780	2296	380	1770	1190	1094	829	1376	521	850	1670	1404	1146	797
Athens	2929	—	3128	1138	2538	2840	1525	3071	2305	1131	2785	4365	2616	3725	2666	2180	2110	3672	2942	2091	2437	3407	1777	2375
Barcelona	1505	3128	—	1799	1283	1309	1935	1309	729	2943	2121	1276	1106	637	484	966	1340	2665	1030	1649	1335	2744	1750	1003
Belgrade	1786	1138	1799	—	1300	1700	385	1934	1353	954	1632	3226	1478	2588	1530	1041	955	2482	1804	953	1482	2255	641	1237
Berlin	665	2538	1283	1300	—	771	1367	941	1070	2254	397	3059	771	2321	1497	1063	575	1185	913	347	1510	1870	663	796
Brussels	220	2840	1309	1700	771	—	1560	193	672	2654	938	2076	222	1550	969	987	762	1539	300	1071	1246	1995	1111	637
Budapest	1401	1525	1935	385	1367	1560	—	1560	1277	938	1247	3172	1189	2533	1476	1049	684	2097	1510	300	1626	2419	312	753
Calais	392	3071	1309	1934	941	193	1560	—	744	2888	1109	2050	422	1524	1034	1312	962	1703	279	1106	1593	2125	1175	641
Geneva	1236	2305	729	1353	1070	672	1277	744	—	2307	1372	1945	489	1303	427	312	585	1962	483	920	889	2253	991	274
Istanbul	2740	1131	2943	954	2254	2654	938	2888	2307	—	2582	4180	2432	3541	2484	1995	1926	3438	2758	1907	2419	3687	1595	2191
Copenhagen	780	2785	2121	1632	397	938	1247	1109	1372	2582	—	2990	989	2464	1796	1502	1087	592	568	1106	1626	312	1614	1206
Lisbon	2296	4365	1276	3226	3059	2076	3172	2050	1945	4180	2990	—	2165	639	1372	2203	2530	3605	2572	2901	2572	3613	2966	2219
Luxembourg	380	2616	1106	1478	771	222	1189	422	489	2432	989	2165	—	1639	792	711	523	1511	339	738	1288	1933	936	415
Madrid	1770	3725	637	2588	2321	1550	2533	1524	1303	3541	2464	639	1639	—	1058	1564	1888	3075	2223	2253	2600	3075	2419	1577
Marseilles	1190	2666	484	1530	1497	969	1476	1034	427	2484	1796	1372	792	1058	—	507	1003	1347	755	876	893	2419	1344	701
Milano	1094	2180	966	1041	1063	987	1049	1312	312	1995	1502	2203	711	1564	507	—	474	711	795	577	577	2125	837	305
Munich	829	2110	1340	955	575	762	684	962	585	1926	1087	2530	523	1888	1003	474	—	1674	832	376	893	1841	422	311
Oslo	1376	3672	2665	2482	1185	1539	2097	1703	1962	3438	592	3605	1511	3075	1347	711	1674	—	1529	977	2600	977	1836	1828
Paris	521	2942	1030	1804	913	300	1510	279	483	2758	568	2572	339	2223	755	795	832	1529	—	738	1372	1372	1399	569
Prague	850	2091	1649	953	347	1071	300	1106	920	1907	1106	2901	738	2253	876	577	376	977	738	—	1288	1399	312	646
Rome	1670	2437	1335	1482	1510	1246	1626	1593	889	2419	1626	2572	1288	2600	893	577	893	2600	1372	1288	—	2610	1614	882
Stockholm	1404	3407	2744	2255	1870	1995	2419	2125	2253	3687	312	3613	1933	3075	2419	2125	1841	977	1372	1399	2610	—	1136	1829
Vienna	1146	1777	1750	641	663	1111	312	1175	991	1595	1614	2966	936	2419	1344	837	422	1836	1399	312	1614	1136	—	733
Zurich	797	2375	1003	1237	796	637	753	641	274	2191	1206	2219	415	1577	701	305	311	1828	569	646	882	1829	733	—

Conversion Table
Kilometers/Miles

A kilometer is 0.621 of a mile. For quick conversion of the kilometers given above, multiply by .6. Example: 100 kilometers equal 60 miles, approximately; actually the figure is 62.1 miles.

Notes

Notes

Notes

Sixty days after graduating from college, Bev Beyer landed in Japan as a US Air Force Service Club director and has been traveling ever since. In 1953 she transferred to Austria as director of the largest US service club in Europe, located in Vienna.

In Vienna she planned transportation, hotel reservations, ski tours and other recreation activities throughout Europe for American servicemen and State Department personnel. Later she was named director of all American service clubs in Italy at the age of 24 and lived in Verona.

During her five years in Europe she began collecting small, comfortable and inexpensive hotels from Oslo to Istanbul for her guide. She is still searching for hotel bargains for her readers and has updated Passport every year since 1960 during her frequent trips to Europe with her travel writer husband, Ed Rabey. They also write a weekly travel column for the *Los Angeles Times*.